the Dream Book

the *Dream Book*

A BEGINNER'S GUIDE TO UNDERSTANDING GOD'S VOICE WHILE YOU SLEEP

STEPHANIE SCHUREMAN

DESTINY IMAGE® PUBLISHERS, INC.

P.O. Box 310, Shippensburg, PA 17257-0310

"Promoting Inspired Lives."

This book and all other Destiny Image and Destiny Image Fiction books are available at Christian bookstores and distributors worldwide.

Cover design by Eileen Rockwell
Interior design by Terry Clifton

For more information on foreign distributors, call 717-532-3040.
Reach us on the Internet: www.destinyimage.com.

ISBN 13 TP: 978-0-7684-1958-0
ISBN 13 eBook: 978-0-7684-1959-7
ISBN 13 HC: 978-0-7684-1961-0
ISBN 13 LP: 978-0-7684-1960-3

For Worldwide Distribution, Printed in the U.S.A.
1 2 3 4 5 6 7 8 / 23 22 21 20 19

Dedication

To the One I love.

Thank You, Jesus, for including me in Your dreams.

To my family from generations past and present, especially my mother, Beth Ann, who have taken their dreams seriously and learned to pray accordingly.

To my children, Candice, Chelsea, Gracie, Caroline, Christian, and Caleb, who tell me their dreams.

To Fire Camp revivalists, both young and mature, from the USA and all over the world. You are the sons and daughters spoken of in Joel 2 and Acts 2. You are listening to how Jesus speaks to you and taking His plan for your lives seriously.

> *This is what I will do in the last days—I will pour out my Spirit on everybody and cause your sons and daughters to prophesy, and your young men will see visions, and your old men will experience dreams from God. The Holy Spirit will come upon all my servants, men and women alike, and they will prophesy* (Acts 2:17-18).

It is our inheritance to dream and a gift from Heaven to understand our dreams.

Acknowledgments

Of the list of wonderful teachers I've been privileged to sit under in the area of dreams, I've received the most influence from my friends Adrian Beale and Adam Thompson, authors of *The Divinity Code to Understanding Your Dreams and Visions*. I want to thank them for how they have pursued God for wisdom and counsel in understanding dreams. I am constantly blessed by the new levels of revelation they receive.

We are blessed in America to have so many excellent teachers to glean from. These have strongly influenced me: John Paul Jackson, Mike Bickle, Lou Engle, Rick Joyner, Jack Hayford, Arthur Burk and, Bill Johnson. I also want to mention beloved pastor James Boulware, who encouraged me to begin reading through my Bible every year, which has been the best foundation for life I could have received.

This book could not have been possible without the help and experience of Fire Camp teachers and participants of all ages.

A special thank you to Janet Freiberg, who has teamed with me to learn and teach dream interpretation to those within our sphere of influence. Her help has been priceless through the process and completion of this book project. I continue to be blessed by how she has humbly but intentionally pursued understanding dreams with Holy Spirit's help.

I want to thank the precious Dwelling Place prayer team members who've been effectively reaching Heaven in prayer for God's answers, direction, and help as this work progressed. You have been vitally instrumental in this project being completed.

Thank you, Nadine Young, precious friend, generous and cheerful distributor of my books in unlikely and hidden places. You are priceless, dear friend. Watching and participating with your obedience to Jesus is always joy!

Thank you, Royalene Doyle, for coaching me out of the "forest of words" and catapulting me to completion.

Thank you to those who've allowed me to publish your private dreams in a public way. Each of you are a valuable part of this project who've shared part of Heaven's "playbook" so we can learn more of Him.

This project was carried on wings of prayer from my own family and joined by many mothers, fathers, relatives, and friends who've been stirred to pray for the spiritual ground to shift toward righteousness in our land. We join our prayers in agreement with Heaven, and with our generations past and present, that the fire of revival will be stirred in us and in the beloved ones we shepherd.

> There are moments in history when a door for massive change opens, and great revolutions for good or evil spring up in the vacuum created by these openings. In these divine moments key men and women and even entire generations risk everything to become the hinge of history, the pivotal point that determines which way the door will swing.
> —Lou Engle, intercessor for revival and co-founder of The Call[1]

[Daniel] could do anything—interpret dreams, solve mysteries, explain puzzles.

—DANIEL 5:12 MSG

The Spirit...dives into the depths of God, and brings out what God planned all along. ...He [Holy Spirit] not only knows what he's [God is] thinking, but he lets us in on it. God offers a full report on the gifts of life and salvation that he is giving us. We don't have to rely on the world's guesses and opinions. We didn't learn this by reading books or going to school; we learned it from God, who taught us person-to-person through Jesus, and we're passing it on to you in the same firsthand, personal way."

—1 CORINTHIANS 2:10-13 MSG

Mummy (Sarah): *"Noah, did you have a dream last night?"*
Noah: *"Yes!"*
Mummy: *"What did you dream about?"*
Noah: *"Jesus!"*
Mummy: *"Reeeally? What did He say to you?"*
Noah: *"I LIKE YOU!"*
—JOHN and SARAH ROTH with their son NOAH, *2½ years old*

Contents

Foreword

Stephanie Schureman's new book, *The Dream Book*, is set to take a new breed of young people into realms beyond this world. With this material God is equipping a generation, who have grown up being fed on fantasy movies and combat games, into their own experience of the supernatural.

God has raised up Stephanie as a prophetic voice to equip young people in a day and age when pioneering minds are searching for something more than empty religious practice.

Like a sleeping giant, the body of Christ is slowly awakening to the fact that dreams and their correct interpretation provide the revelation needed to step beyond church rhetoric to the substance of the Kingdom of God, "For the Kingdom of God is not in word, but in power." Sadly, most do not realize there is a very real game of thrones underway in the unseen eternal realm and that to fight a spiritual foe you need spiritual weapons.

Through this book, Yeshua, our Lord and Commander is setting forth the real call of duty to a corporate body of young people to take up the baton filled with the Presence of God and knowledge of the gifts of the Spirit to fulfill their destiny and shine like the stars forever.

ADAM F. THOMPSON and ADRIAN BEALE
Authors of *The Divinity Code to Understanding Your Dreams*
and *Visions and God's Prophetic Symbolism in Everyday Life*

I had a dream two nights ago.

We were in a stadium with tens of thousands of Christians. Moms, dads, grandparents, and lots of children. It was beautiful! Lots of families enjoying themselves, and I was one of the speakers for this Christian event.

The speaker before me was quite old and somewhat careless with her words. I was surprised that she was not more careful with what she was saying. Then I heard her say about all the kids who were there, "Children are to be seen and not heard."

My heart was so heavy as the faces of the children present flashed before me; they were hurt, deeply hurt. Then it was my turn to take the mic and I simply said, "The children **must** be heard! The children have a **voice** that must be heard!"

I then knelt down in front of one child after another and looked into their eyes and said, "You have a voice for this day. You have a voice that must be heard." I awoke with the strong sense that we are on the verge of a "children's revival."

The praises of our children have the power to silence the voice of the enemy. May the children's voices be heard in our land again!

—DR. BRIAN SIMMONS, Author of *The Passion Translation*

You have built a stronghold by the songs of babies. Strength rises up with the chorus of singing children. This kind of praise has the power to shut Satan's mouth. Childlike worship will silence the madness of those who oppose you (Psalm 8:2).

Preface

First, I'd like to share the encounter with Jesus that has brought this book assignment into my life.

While volunteering at our county library's warehouse, I was given the job of sorting children's books into general categories. With stacks and stacks of books to organize, I was sorting as fast as possible so the books were passing through my hands quite quickly.

Suddenly, I was stopped by a noticeable *physical electric jolt* that seemed to originate from one of the books that had passed through my hands. I stopped, retrieved the book that had brought on the jolt, and took a break from my work. With the book in hand, I went outside to talk to Jesus about what was on His mind concerning this book.

I scanned the table of contents and book description, learning that the book written for young children and was about night dreams and how to interpret dreams. The message was from a humanistic perspective, with lots of new age terminology. The basis for interpreting their dreams was considered "a magical process" where they could hear from "another (somewhat mysterious) realm." The author was defining dream metaphors and the supernatural from a secular viewpoint, leaving God, the Creator of both dreams and the supernatural, completely out of the picture.

I've been in love with Jesus my entire life. His Word has come alive in me. For over a decade, I have had the great joy of teaching people of all ages Fire

Camp, which is practical training on how to hear God's voice and interpret dreams. With my whole heart I believe dreams are an amazing gift from a loving God, and the interpretation, wisdom, and strategy that He is delivering has our absolute best in mind.

Just as you go to the instruction manual written by the creator of a device to learn how to correctly use the product, shouldn't we ask the Author and Creator of dreams for the true and relevant interpretation?

I began to search for available good alternatives to the secular dream book and was surprised by the lack of resources for the believing young person. Most of the resources available were either new age, psychology/humanistic based, or worse.

Thus the "God assignment" to write this book became my next adventure. If it was His idea, I was confident He would speak through this willing but weak and naïve vessel. Young people are on Jesus's mind. It is His turn to have an opportunity to define the supernatural from His perspective, using His Word and with His best intentions and matchless love in mind. This book is not just a resource but a point of encounter with the Creator and Interpreter of all dreams. The dream realm was His first, and it is ours to have Kingdom authority in—the great tool of this day and for the great harvest in our future.

All so the Lamb that was slain will receive the full reward of His suffering.

With much joy and anticipation of His Kingdom being established,
STEPHANIE SCHUREMAN

Introduction to Parents

I was sitting in an office, filling out building rental paperwork for an upcoming dream conference we were hosting. The topic of conversation turned to a dream the event manager, Shirley, had just had early that morning.

In her dream, Shirley found herself walking through a strikingly beautiful home surrounded by things she loves. She knew this house was hers! She was overwhelmed by the beautiful components of the home and amazed at the attention to detail and the obvious love someone had shown for her in taking on this project. It was as if the person who built this beautiful home knew her preferences better than she knew them herself.

Shirley was surprised to see treasured items from her childhood. Even the beloved pets she cherished in her life were there waiting for her. Shirley was puzzled by the dream but was overwhelmed by the love she had felt.

Interpretation

My meeting with Shirley was not a coincidence. As gently as possible, I explained how God had given her this dream to remind her of His love and care for her. That He knows every detail of her life *even better* than she knows herself. He wants her to see a glimpse of her heavenly home. He is pursuing real relationship (not just church) with her and offering the reality and beauty of Heaven, not only after she dies but today!

Shirley listened politely to me then related how her daughter (who dreams all the time) goes to a psychic to get her dreams interpreted.

Our conversation ended with me encouraging her to seek out the truth of her dreams from God because He deeply loves her and has the very best plan for her.

I believe Jesus was allowing Shirley a glimpse of Heaven. He is in pursuit of a deeper relationship with her.

> *Move your heart closer and closer **to God**, and*
> *He will come even closer **to you*** (James 4:8).

In our culture, science, psychology, or "enlightened thought" have been given the bulk of influence in defining the supernatural and its use without considering or consulting the Creator of the supernatural realm.

When a scientist makes a discovery, he is asked to give more information of what he has learned and many times is required to present findings so all can benefit. Today, our culture avoids considering the Creator's thoughts on the realm of the supernatural. Those who practice the counterfeit are readily accepted as relevant, *"always learning but never discover the revelation-knowledge of truth"* (2 Tim. 3:7).

The recent influx of popular literature seeking to teach our young people how to operate in the supernatural without godly wisdom is not only troubling but dangerous. This ideology is devastating lives, fracturing homes, and brutalizing our culture. You can go to any bookstore and see numerous titles that train young people to operate in sorcery, witchcraft, and every imaginable variation possible.

The church (in general) has answered this problem in a confusing way; some even embrace this supernatural instruction as "entertainment" and harmless. Second Timothy 3:1,5 says, "*in the final days the culture of society…may pretend to have a respect for God, but in reality they want nothing to do with God's power. Stay away from people like these!*"

We Have the Best Tools!

Jesus gave the command to His disciples to take the gospel to the world, but He commanded them to *first* wait for the gift of the Holy Spirit. Not only did He give us the best tools to share Jesus, He demands we use these tools (see Acts 1:4,8; 1 Cor. 12).

> *I will pour out of My Spirit on **all flesh**; your **sons and your daughters** shall prophesy, your **young** men shall **see visions**, your **old** men shall **dream dreams**. And on My menservants and on My maidservants I **will pour out My Spirit in those days*** (Acts 2:17-18 NKJV).

The key to lasting revival among our young people is setting them on a foundation of God's Word that does not *deny them access to* or *ignore* the true biblical supernatural.

It is my prayer that this book will be a resource to help train believers (of all ages) in true, life-changing, enjoyable, and safe dream interpretation, as well as bring godly wisdom to the supernatural gifts and experiences.

The goal of this book is to consistently point to Scripture as the first and ultimate source of making dream interpretation accessible.

Notes

Joseph said to them, "God is the only One who can explain the meaning of dreams" (Genesis 40:8 ICB).

Training Young Believers in Understanding Their Dreams

In this book, most chapters begin with a dream or experience that draws the reader into the learning process and gently compels them not only to *read* but *to dwell on the Word of God*. This will give excellent understanding and open up brilliant revelation in their own dreams with Holy Spirit's guidance. As God's Word is sown into their heart and mind, they will come to understand His love and good plans for them. His excellence and truth will become their high standard and they will never be compelled or satisfied by an inferior or unrighteous source.

In life, I have tried to model real relationship with Jesus and His Word before my family as honestly as possible (definitely not perfectly), believing this foundation will keep them from *permanently* departing from God. However, if they choose to stray for a time I am confident in the *powerful and effective Word of God* teamed with *Holy Spirit* to compel them back into the safe arms of Jesus. I believe, when our young ones have been raised in a Spirit-led environment,t will be difficult to find contentment in whatever may temporarily capture their attention.

I choose to trust the work of the Holy Spirt in our young people's lives, that when they step out of Jesus's protection they'll quickly recognize that chaos has interrupted true peace and that settling for inferior things of this world will never satisfy. My prayer is that every child of God will continually crave the living, breathing,

Once you've encountered Jesus and His power, you'll never be content with less than another encounter of His love.

vibrant, and healthy food of God's Word they've been blessed to feast on.

In the above dream experience, it was difficult for me to hear Shirley say that her beloved daughter uses a psychic to interpret her dreams. This is our assignment as the true church. We must take up our positions as excellent teachers of the prophetic and interpreters of dreams so that hearts are impacted by the Holy Spirit and His truth and Jesus's Word becomes water to those who are thirsty after truth.

My goal is to team up with the active and living church, opening up God's true supernatural gifts and revelatory wisdom, making simple what has seemed impossible or too difficult. We, as believers in God's Word have access to answers—abundantly available—in the precious Word of God and the amazing Holy Spirit, who guides us into all truth.

> *Don't forget all that has been deposited within you. Escape from the empty echoes of men and the perversion of twisted reasoning. For those who claim to possess this so-called knowledge have already wandered from the true faith. May God's grace empower you always!*
> (1 Timothy 6:20-21)

Remembering Heaven

As in the dream at the beginning of this section, a dream may bring memories of Heaven. It has been said that a child may be able to recall details or thoughts of Heaven up to about two and a half or three years of age.

Notes

"Please tell me about Heaven, I'm starting to forget."

—Three-year-old to his younger
sister standing in her crib

While we were cooking dinner, Lucie, almost three years old, stopped and stared at a picture of a lighthouse on a jar of dressing and said, "Remember when I used to live in the lighthouse?"

Then, as she continued to ponder this thought, she asked, "Mom, where was I when I was in the lighthouse?"

Mom and Grammie both knew she had not been in an earthly lighthouse or even understood what one was, but realized she was probably remembering Heaven.

—Stephanie, with daughter Gracie
and granddaughter Lucie

While lying in bed with two-year-old Christian, I (Lisa) asked him if he remembered Heaven. Christian said, "Yes, I was sad."

"Really? Why were you sad?"

"Because Daddy came and put me in your belly."

"Well, where were you before you were in my belly?"

Christian said, "With Jesus."

"What were you doing?"

"He (Jesus) was singing to me."

Then Christian started singing this song that was like nothing I had ever heard. I want to say it was similar to singing in tongues, but it doesn't clearly articulate how it sounded.

"Was anyone else there with you?" I said.

"A boy and a girl. They knew my name." And then he started to describe what they looked like.

I (Lisa) have two babies in Heaven—a boy, Daniel, and a girl, Isabelle, whom Christian did not know about yet. I just wept. It was such a gift from God to let me know they are with Jesus.

When I saw the movie *Heaven Is for Real*, it was confirming to me that Colton and Christian had similar experiences in Heaven. Rainbow horses, siblings. Christian chuckles now when we talk about this because those memories have faded, but that season strengthened our faith more than any other time.

—Memory shared by LISA CARON, mom of Christian

Before I shaped you in the womb, I knew all about you. Before you saw the light of day, I had holy plans for you (Jeremiah 1:5 MSG).

Long before he laid down earth's foundations, he had us in mind, had settled on us as the focus of his love, to be made whole and holy by his love. Long, long ago he decided to adopt us into his family through Jesus Christ. (What pleasure he took in planning this!) (Ephesians 1:4 MSG).

Notes

Basic Understanding of Dream Interpretation

Opportunity to Hear
from Heaven

1:   God; beginning; source; first in order, time, rank, or importance; love; first heaven (earthly, physical realm, see 2 Cor. 12:2-4).[2]

I cannot escape.

My thoughts are drifting.
Eyes too heavy to hold open.
This story begins.
In my dream, a "digital man" has risen to power. He knows details about me, my friends, and my family. He knows my cell-phone number, my address, details about my life. This digital man is able to control how I spend money, what I buy at the store.
This makes me feel unsafe.
He is dark. The sky is dark. He has power over everyone I know.
The dream ends, I wake up.
—Caleb, age 9

A Unique Opportunity to Hear from Heaven

As your body sleeps, your mind is quiet. Things that normally distract you are absent. God has this moment and your full attention. Jesus, the ultimate Storywriter, spins a tale that interweaves details from your life including people you are familiar with into a fascinating story line to captivate your imagination.

KEY: The dream story may highlight an area of your life, help you solve a problem, or give you a different perspective on a decision you are about to make or a relationship you are currently in.

That Dream Was Weird!

Most dreams are a bit bizarre. As friends tell you their dreams, you get used to hearing some odd and unusual scenarios, some of which may be very funny. A dream is like a parable incorporating components from daily life and culture to convey a concept you would not have thought of on your own.

Caleb's dream at the beginning of this chapter is a good example of a parable dream. It tells a story, addresses an issue, and leaves the dreamer seeking an interpretation. As simple as the dream may seem, its message is quite profound.

The goal of interpretation is to catch the message of the dream to help the dreamer gain wisdom and work for positive change in his life.

The Basic Process of Dream Interpretation

Let's revisit Caleb's dream and the various elements it contains.

> *"In my dream, a 'digital man' has risen to power."*

- In real life, Caleb has allowed himself to be influenced by the "digital man."

QUESTION: Who is this "digital man"?

> *"He knows details about me, my friends, and my family. He knows my cell phone number, my address, details about my life."*

- The *digital man* knows how to communicate with Caleb by way of technology such as cell phone, text, pictures, video, etc. These are various means by which the dreamer communicates with others in actual life.

- The digital man is using those *forms of communication* to influence Caleb.

- The digital man knows where Caleb lives and has access to his *home*. In this case, "home" represents the dreamer's life or heart. (See Luke 12:34.)

- The digital man has *access to details* in Caleb's life and his heart.

- This dream is alerting the dreamer, either positively or negatively, to what or who has access into your heart.

WHAT TO DO WHEN YOU HAVE A DREAM

1. Write or record the dream.

2. Ask God to help you understand what the dream means.

3. Repeat the entire dream to yourself or to a friend.

4. Define some of the metaphors in the dream.

5. Retell the dream story with the understanding you've received.

Notes

QUESTION: When you woke did you feel at peace or fearful about the person who had access to you?

ANSWER: When Caleb woke, he was fearful about the dream. This helps us answer the question about whether the intent of the influencer in the dream is good or evil. His intent is not good for Caleb.

> *"The digital man is able to control how I spend money, what I buy at the store."*

- It seems the digital man has some amount of *control* or influence in the dreamer's life, thoughts, and actions.

- *Control* represents authority and is influencing how the dreamer uses his time, money, and abilities.

- In a dream, money may represent what is valuable to the dreamer. What you spend money on is what you treasure (see Matt. 6:19-21).

> *"This makes me feel unsafe. He is dark. The sky is dark."*

Feelings are important *clues* on how a dream is to be interpreted. In Caleb's dream:

- Clue 1: The digital man causes the dreamer to feel unsafe.

- Clue 2: The digital man *is dark*.

Notes

- Clue 3: The sky is *dark*.

When a dream is dark or has an uneasy feeling about it, the common assumption is to believe that the enemy is speaking. However, you should never go to the enemy for answers or interpretation of any dream, for the enemy is a liar (see John 8:42-44).

The Bible makes it very clear that all true dream interpretation belongs to God (see Gen. 40:8; Dan. 2:26-28). The digital man is "dark"—simply put, he is the enemy. God knows what is in darkness, and He exposes it! (See Daniel 2:22.)

Does the enemy want you to know his plans against you? No.

Does Jesus want you to see the enemy's plans? Yes!

Instead of assuming the enemy sent the above dream, let's focus on what Jesus is revealing in it. Jesus works for our success and will always *expose the enemy's plans* against us, revealing the *strategy* to defeat him. God does not give us a spirit of fear, but He may allow us to experience the fear the enemy's plan will produce. God wants to give you the confidence needed to defeat the enemy.

> *"He (digital man or enemy) has power over everyone I know."*

- This enemy may be influencing Caleb's friends, family, and his community in general.

- Even if others follow the digital man, it is not safe for Caleb to be under his influence.

- What message did Jesus want to convey from the clues and elements in Caleb's dream?

This dream is a good warning.

Caleb was given the dream so he would be able to recognize that he is in danger of allowing the digital man to have too much influence in his life through gaming, videos, or other forms of media.

- Digital media can be good if used properly and with healthy boundaries.

- The above dream may serve as a warning for Caleb that he should not hand over control to something or someone that will bring about loss of freedom and peace.

The Extraordinary Gift of Free Will

God will do as much as possible—without taking away our *free will*—to keep us from being taken advantage of by the enemy. We have freedom to make the decision to listen to and *hear* the instruction of a dream or ignore its message. God will never overstep the gift of free will He has given to us.

Dreams are an invitation to hear and partner with Heaven's wisdom. Jesus will go to whatever lengths necessary to build friendship with you. He has seen where you are and where you will be. He is waiting for an invitation to be on the journey with you so that He may equip you with wisdom and creativity to accomplish all you were made for. To Jesus, you are a history maker! He is looking forward, with much joy, to making this journey with you!

The Ramp, the Runway

2: Witness (agreement); testimony; reward; support (like friendship); twins; double blessing; second heaven (see Eph. 6:12).

*We were at camp somewhere in central India with over 100 young people. Sandeep, our interpreter, drowsy because of lack of sleep, was working hard to stay awake **while doing the difficult work of translating** for our Fire Camp teachers.*

Then the most amazing thing happened.

Sandeep woke, startled that he had continued to translate in his sleep!

Neither the teacher nor students realized what had happened, because the translation from English to Telugu and back to English was seamless!

This is how good God is. Not only is He a linguist, He can put our physical body to sleep and translate His thoughts through us while we rest, while we dream.

Just one of the language miracles we experienced in travel.

Metaphors Simplified

Communication is never a problem with God. He understands not only your spoken language, He understands every single detail about your history, how you think, and why you process life as you do. He communicates by using a multitude of language tools. He will speak in words common to you by using pictures, numbers, colors, and stories that describe His thoughts.

Learning to "hear" God's thoughts is similar to understanding a language that is in your native tongue but with a different form of transmission. For example, American Sign Language is based upon English but is "spoken" with hand signals and difficult to understand unless you are familiar with this form of transmission.

Word Pictures = Metaphors = Parables

It seems that word pictures or metaphors are Jesus's favorite tool to help you understand His thoughts. Word pictures cross language, culture, thought, and religious barriers and can giving us a common language with God.

Parables were Jesus's favorite teaching tool to use whenever He taught on earth. A dream is a parable given in your sleep.

We use the term *metaphor* to identify something we recognize from our own life and bring a spiritual meaning or lesson to. When you compare the metaphor to Scripture you gain more understanding of how to interpret the dream.

How a Metaphor Helps You Understand a Dream

- An *airport runway* is a pathway for an airplane to take off or land.

- Using *runway* as a metaphor, a runway represents a pathway to a "higher" realm, a heavenly realm where God dwells.

- When we ask God for His understandings it is similar to using a *runway* to launch us into His Presence.

- A *runway* is also defined as a *beaten path* or type of *land bridge* that people (or animals) take to quickly get from one place to another. This is a metaphor (picture) of how we take *the beaten path, the well-used path,* or *the bridge* of God's Word to develop understanding of a dream by talking to Him in prayer. This *bridge* connects us to His thoughts about our life.

- An *entrance ramp* is the way our motor vehicles get onto the highway. Used as a metaphor, we understand this "High-way" is the higher way of understanding and accessing the Spirit of God. You may also see this represented as a *high* school or a place of "higher" learning.

- If you dream that you are walking, riding a bike or skateboard, or moving in any form of vehicle onto an onramp, you are seeing how God is helping you to "come up" to a *higher understanding* of His thoughts.

These metaphor examples in a dream give us understanding of how a dream actually works. God uses word-picture metaphors to take us to a higher place so we can understand His thoughts about us. I cannot know what

Notes

The disciples would ask, "What are You talking about, Jesus?" because they were trying to grasp His thoughts with their natural minds without accessing the Spirit of God.

Notes

A key to understanding dreams is to recognize that **all dreams and interpretation** come from God (see Gen. 40:8); we must depend on His Spirit for interpretation.

Jesus is thinking unless I access God's Spirit (see 1 Cor. 2:14-16).

A dream is like receiving an invitation to hear what God thinks of a current situation in our life.

This is huge!

The God of the heavens and of earth cares about even the simplest details of our life and will give us a scenario in our dreams to speak to us about our thoughts, actions, plans, decisions, and relationships.

Think about how priceless you are to God. He takes the time to "write" a script and then allow the parable dream/vision to play out on a stage in your mind while you sleep, all so you can "see" how He thinks about your life and learn His perspective.

When asked why He always spoke to people in hard-to-understand parables, Jesus explained:

> *You've been given the intimate experience of insight into the **hidden truths** and **mysteries of the realm of heaven's kingdom**, but they have not. For everyone who listens with an open heart will receive progressively more **revelation** until he has more than enough* (Matthew 13:11-12).

The Ancient Book of Dreams

3: God (Father, Son, and Holy Spirit); perfect; Holy Spirit; three items may be three days or three years; third heaven (where God dwells).

> *Listen to this dream I had. We were all out in the field gathering bundles of wheat. All of a sudden my bundle stood straight up and your bundles circled around it and bowed down to mine.*
>
> *I dreamed another dream—the sun and moon and 11 stars bowed down to me!*
> —JOSEPH, age 17

Did Ancient People Understand Their Dreams?

Yes, they did.

Joseph, whose dream is quoted above, was the second youngest member of his family. When Joseph told these dreams to his brothers an uproar ensued in his family. They understood that dreams were messages from God and perceived the dreams would come to pass even though they could not see how.

Joseph must have been a prolific dreamer. Most of his life was directed by dreams. Instead of running from God or blaming God for his difficult circumstances, Joseph learned how God was speaking to him and chose to gain wisdom from his dreams. His relationship with God grew deeper and his dream interpretation skills were profound.

Eventually, the two dreams quoted above came true and were vital to the rescue of Joseph's family (whose descendants would become the nation of Israel). The dreams were key to Joseph's success. The wisdom he had attained from his relationship with God gave him the ability to sustain the entire nation of Egypt through deadly famine (see Gen. 37, 39–50).

A dream may keep you from losing hope in difficult circumstances.

Instead of Joseph's brothers congratulating him for the dreams he received from God, they were angry and jealous and caused him much pain. He was even rebuked by his father, who nonetheless kept the dream's message in mind (see Gen. 37:11). Regardless of how Joseph was treated and the difficulty he endured, Joseph learned to place his confidence in God.

Like Joseph, you are designed to impact the earth.

You were not placed here by accident or happenstance; rather, God has allowed you to be born into the right place and time. You were made in the likeness of God and created with an aspect of God's nature that no one else can duplicate or operate in. You carry tremendous potential.

When God created you, He created a dream and wrapped a body around it. —Lou Engle

Can I Learn to Interpret Dreams?

Absolutely, yes.

I believe God would not give dreams if He did not expect to help us understand them.

By far, the most important key to understanding dreams is the relationship you build with the One who gives dreams. The time you spend talking to Jesus, getting familiar with His Word, and simply understanding how He speaks is priceless.

Make it your goal to understand your dreams from His eyes. When you take this step, He helps you gain His perspective of your life.

> *Trust in the Lord completely, and do not rely on your own opinions. With all your heart rely on him to guide you, and he will lead you in every decision you make. ...Don't think for a moment that you know it all, for wisdom comes when you adore him* (Proverbs 3:5-7 TPT).

Holy Spirit holds the key.

A dream that is difficult to understand is similar to a padlock that has been fastened. Not just any key will open the lock. Not just any interpretation will open your heart to understand the meaning.

The *lock* represents your heart (see Prov. 4:23). The metal tumblers inside the lock stay scrambled and keep revelation from being unlocked to the dreamer.

Notes

Notes

When Holy Spirit brings true revelation to a dream, it is like the key that aligns the tumblers of the lock and the lock pops open! The truth Holy Spirit reveals fills your heart with joy and purpose. The *key* represents authority, opportunity, and access (see Prov. 25:2).

God University

4: Rule; the earth or the physical; direction, as in north, east, south, and west; creation; spirit realm or time as in the fourth dimension; Jesus as the fourth man in the furnace.

> I dreamed that I was driving my car and going quite fast. The problem was, I could not open my eyes! I could not see where I was going!
>
> —TERESA

God University

You, your physical body, your soul (mind, will, and emotions), and your spirit (connection to God) are the subject of most of your dreams. God is the best teacher you can possibly want to learn from because He sees the big picture of your life—your past, present, and future.

A dream is an invitation to attend your own personal "God University." The subject of each class is *you!* Course development continues through your life with God's perspective of your circumstances—good and difficult, from conception to when you leave this life to join Him in Heaven. At the core of this study is God's very best plan for your life, focused with His perfect love.

Interpretation of the dream above:

A *car* or any vehicle can be a representation of your own heart. Being *unable to open your eyes*—driving down a street but not being able to see where you are going—is like approaching life without God's view of your circumstances.

In the above dream, Teresa experienced, in parable form, what it is like to live without spiritual vision. God is letting her know He wants to "open her spiritual eyes" so she can gain His perspective, which will lead to success.

When you step back and look at your situation, ask God to help you see the lesson He is teaching through each dream. A single dream can be like a new chapter in your personal textbook, assigned so that you can pursue the Teacher (Holy Spirit) for understanding of the subject.

God is motivated to help you excel in this classroom.

A dream may be extremely personal. Our actions, thoughts, attitudes, and intentions are completely visible to God. God is not embarrassed of you, about you, or by you—ever! He is very pleased at how He made you. He knows when and where you need to mature so that your gifts are useful and you can accomplish all He has called you to.

Be an excellent student. Stay humble; keep practicing hearing what God is saying to you. Stay close to His Word so you can learn all the wisdom you can without need to retake the test.

> *In a dream, for instance, a vision at night, when men and women are deep in sleep, fast asleep in their beds—God **opens their ears***

*and impresses them with **warnings** to **turn them back from something bad they're planning**, from some **reckless choice**, and keep them from an **early grave**, from the river of no return* (Job 33:15-18 MSG).

A repetitive dream is important because Jesus is looking for permission to deal with a particular issue OR the dream is going to come true shortly. In either case, pay close attention to repetitive dreams.

And the dream **was repeated** to Pharaoh twice because the thing is established by God, and God will shortly bring it to pass. (Genesis 41:32 NKJV)

What happens if I make the wrong choice? Does God see me as a failure?

Quite the opposite.

God never sees you as a failure but, rather, is giving you the path to learn wisdom. He gives you the opportunity to retake the test as many times as needed. You may re-dream the same dream over and over.

God does not override your free-will choices.

He is persistent.

His love is immeasurable.

When you make a mistake or do not pass a test, run to Him and ask for His help. He is working for your success.

Script-ure

ς: Grace, abundance, favor.

> I was swimming as fast as possible downstream a rapidly moving river. Someone was chasing me!
>
> Turning to see who was behind, I realized it was a one-year-old calf! The cow was coming up behind me fast, so I struggled to swim faster. Then I realized he was laughing hilariously!
>
> Working hard to swim faster, laughter overtook me because of the situation.
>
> Finding a calm place on the river bank, I climbed out of the rushing river and escaped the cow by jumping over a fence. Much to my surprise, the cow got out of the river and jumped the fence behind me. The cow and I fell on the ground laughing hysterically.
>
> When I woke, I immediately heard the words, "Cash cow!"
>
> —Steph

We are not handed a script for life, but "Script-ure" is the Director's notes.

Every motion picture or play has a script, complete with characters and personality traits that help bring a story to life. When you have a dream, realize you've just heard from the One and Only most brilliant Scriptwriter and

Director of your life and you have permission to ask for clarification of His thoughts.

God will reveal information in a dream or vision that you could not possibly know in the natural. He sees the big picture and is giving you access to the script.

God may use a metaphor that will make you laugh.

The metaphor "cash cow" would not have been a normal thought in my mind. If I had not heard the Spirit speak clearly outside of my own understanding, I may have missed God's thought on the dream. God used this particular metaphor because He knew I would understand it as provision. The dream has given me confidence to trust the Lord when it seemed in the natural there was not enough "cash" or provision available. This was God's tricky way to help me agree and declare with Philippians 4:19 which promises that *He will supply* all of my needs according to His riches.

Since having this dream, my vocabulary has changed to include the metaphor "cash cow." I catch myself exclaiming in agreement with this dream and with Scripture, "I have a cash cow!" This dream made me catch God's promise and apply it in a more substantial way in my own life.

Learning God's language

God loves to use every form of literary tool to stretch us and get us to pursue Him for answers. He'll use puns, humor, double meanings of words or names, even a common saying like *cash cow* that is personally known but in the dream it takes on a whole new meaning.

Notes

Notes

The list of methods used to convey Jesus's thoughts about us is limitless.

Parable: A simple story to help understand a profound truth. Typically, a parable in a dream uses surroundings, culture, people, and various items (e.g., bicycles, animals/bugs, plants, numbers) common to daily life.

Riddle: A game, puzzle, or hidden truth designed to be found out by unraveling a mysterious, contradictory statement or picture. A riddle causes one to pursue answers that have been intentionally hidden.

Enigma: Even this word's definition is a bit ambiguous. Sometimes dreams are unexplainable. We may receive partial understanding but be stymied at a contradiction. It can be baffling when full revelation is not readily available. I've learned to be content knowing that God's thoughts and ways are far above mine (see Isa. 55:8-9).

I don't need to know everything.

> The secret things belong to the Lord our God, but those things which are revealed belong to us and to our children (Deuteronomy 29:29 NKJV).

The meaning of a dream may become clear as time passes or one or more events take place. Finding the interpretation of a dream is a blessing and a gift. God does not promise to give us a full interpretation every single time, but we can be confident that He will give us information as we need it.

God wants to speak to you firsthand.

God uses dreams to speak to us when we are asleep because *our reasoning and defenses to hearing a new or neglected concept are disabled.* Suddenly, we are available to hear His thoughts in a fresh way. In the above dream the concept of God's provision had been understood, but after having the dream, a new level of confidence in His provision was stirred up.

God speaks in story or parable language, a riddle, or an enigma so that the dreamer will pursue the interpretation and ultimately find and build and strengthen our relationship with Him.

Such is God's intense, consuming love for His children. It's a love that knows no limits and no boundaries. A love that will go to any lengths, and take any risks, to pursue us. —Brennan Manning, *The Furious Longing of God*

I am all he wants. I'm all the world to him (Song of Solomon 7:10 MSG).

Notes

Isaac 0111, My New Address

6: **Number of man, created on the sixth day; number of the prophet; rest (six days brings us to rest).**

Not long ago, I had a dream. In that dream, I arrived at my house, but when I looked at the address it had changed. This was clearly my house, but my address was now Isaac 0111. This sent me on an exciting search that went like this:

The concept of *metaphor* and my own general *knowledge* taught me that:

- *Isaac* means "laughter."

- In the Bible, Isaac was a favored son, in covenant with God—a son of freedom, not a slave.

- Isaac was born when his father, Abraham, was 100 years old.

- The number 100 represents "complete, full blessing."

- The idea of my home address represents the place where I live and/or where my heart is.

- The number zero can represent God or possibly in this case having *no agenda* or "to-do list" for God—simply abiding with Him.

- One, one, one: The first letter of the Hebrew alphabet is *aleph*, which actually consists of three parts but has the numeric value of one. It is symbolic of God, the Three-in-One. God, the compound unity—Father, Son, and Holy Spirit.

An *Internet search* produced the following thoughts:

- 0111 is 1:11 A.M. military time. This did not mean anything in particular to me, but the search is fun and interesting.

- The US Department of Labor has labeled "wheat farming" with the numbers 0111. To me, this represents the harvest that Jesus talks about in the Bible, where many people come to know Jesus. My life work is to partner with Jesus in this (see Matt. 10:5-8).

- In binary code, the number 0111 equals 7. When seeking to interpret a dream/ message and a number is repeated, pay close attention because it is God highlighting something important. God speaks in every language. No code, language, formula, or system is unknown or hidden from Him.

In a *Scripture search* I found that 0111 was the designation given to a very specific piece of Scripture recorded on a fragile parchment, written in uncial or very small capital letters. This is the passage we know today as Second Thessalonians 1:1–2:2, and the uncial copy dates from the seventh century. The Scripture and numbers associated with it, including the number 7 (rest and completion), were very meaningful, timely, and beloved to me, personally.

Our Bibles today use a numbered system we can easily follow. Here are two possible Scripture examples from 111.

> *May the Lord, the God of your fathers, add to you a thousand times as many as you are and bless you, just as He has promised you!* (Deuteronomy 1:11 AMP)

> *Where can wisdom be found? It is born in the fear of God. Everyone who follows his ways will never lack his living-understanding* (Psalm 111:10).

Isaac 0111: A Type of Riddle Dream

The reason this dream stuck in my memory so well is because the address started with zero, which does not happen in reality. The number triggered my attention toward God's thoughts.

I knew I had to solve the riddle, and that quest took me to places of understanding I would not have captured had I not pursued His thoughts. Not all of what I found in my research applied to the dream interpretation, but the search for what Jesus may be saying is captivating and fun.

Because the dream so clearly showed me an address that I *knew* was my home address, I also realized it had to do with me and what was going on in my own heart. Jesus *knew right where I lived* and what *I needed to know* even better than I did myself. He gave me the dream in order to encourage me as well as remind me how much He cares about the details of my life.

Notes

You will have a unique understanding of your dreams and clever ideas of how to search and study the metaphors in your dreams.

I am content with the encouragement found from the above searches. Keeping in mind that Jesus may reveal more, I'm *listening* to Him to reveal why He has named my earthly home Isaac 0111.

> *God conceals the revelation of his word in the hiding place of his glory. But the honor of kings is revealed by how they thoroughly search out the deeper meaning of all that God says* (Proverbs 25:2).

Notes

Do I Have to Believe in God to Get a Dream from God?

7: Divine perfection; rest; completion; blessed; satisfied; seven days or years; seven days in a week; seven colors in a rainbow (promise); the musical scale.

No, it does not matter if the dreamer is a believer in God or not.

Everyone has the ability to receive dreams from God. From ancient times to the present we have stories from people of all age groups, professions, and belief systems not only dreaming but giving credit to God for their dreams.

> *He [God] is kind to all by bringing the sunrise to warm and rainfall to refresh whether a person does what is good or evil* (Matthew 5:45).

Ancient Dreamers

One of the oldest examples of an unbeliever receiving a dream is recorded in the book of Genesis. The man's name is Abimelech, the king of Gerar, a very ancient town at the southern border of Israel.

Abraham, a friend of God, traveled to a country where *unrighteous* King Abimelech was the ruler. Abraham, fearing the king may kill him so that he could take Sarah as his own wife, chose to tell King Abimelech that Sarah was only his sister. Sarah was very beautiful. Abimelech, not knowing Sarah was already married to Abraham, invited her into his palace, intending to soon take her as his own wife.

God kept Sarah safe in the king's palace, and that night Abimelech received a powerful warning dream from God. Even though Abimelech did not yet serve God, God was merciful to him and gave him very specific information. Because of the dream, Abimelech returned Sarah to Abraham and the king was preserved from certain death. This dream helped align both the king and Abraham with God's plan.

The dream and events just spoken of are found in Genesis 20—one of the earliest historical records of a dream. I encourage you to take time and read the entire story.

The Dream Vehicle

A dream is a vehicle that God uses to convey His ideas, thoughts, and plans to whomever He chooses, no matter what religious belief or experience we have. *Nothing deters His ability to get our attention.*

God searches out every person, from the very youngest to the very oldest, from the nicest person to the one who has done everything wrong. No one is too far away or can hide from His love. He uses a dream to go to anywhere on the planet to speak to one person.

In a dream, God can communicate to us in such a unique and captivating way that no matter what belief system we are born into or have developed, we will be compelled to

Notes

search for this One who knows and loves every tiny detail about us.

Remember: The dream is similar to a vehicle. Once on board the dream vehicle, you use the "on-ramp" or "runway" to go to a higher place to gain higher understanding of God's thoughts.

> *For as the heavens are **higher** than the earth,*
> *so are My ways **higher** than your ways and*
> *My thoughts **higher** than your thoughts*
> (Isaiah 55:9 AMP).

The Brilliant Source
of Wisdom

8:   **New beginning; superabundant; super-strength; infinity or eternity.**

George Washington Carver, the famous researcher, botanist, and inventor of Tuskegee Institute, has been called the world's greatest biochemist. He is best known for his discovery of hundreds of valuable uses for the sweet potato and the peanut, including soap, paper, glue, and medicine.

In 1921, Dr. Carver was invited to testify before the United States Senate Ways and Means Committee on the possibilities of the peanut. Initially given only ten minutes to speak, he so captivated the committee that the chairman said, "Go ahead, Brother. Your time is unlimited."

Carver spoke for one hour and 45 minutes. At the conclusion of his presentation the chairman asked, "Dr. Carver, how did you learn all of these things?"

Carver replied, "From an old Book."

"What book?" the senator queried.

The famed scientist replied, "The Bible."

"Does the Bible tell about peanuts?" the surprised senator inquired.

"No, sir," Dr. Carver replied, "but it tells about the God who made the peanut. I asked Him to show me what to do with the peanut, and He did."

The Bible was Dr. Carver's single source of truth.

Just as George Washington Carver understood the best Source to learn about the peanut, I want to point you to the single best source for understanding dreams and dream interpretation—the Bible.

This unusual but brilliant Book is unmatched in bringing wisdom and understanding on a vast number of subjects to people and nations from earliest history to the present. You can study the Bible for the rest of your life and never exhaust its content.

> *The Word was first, the Word present to God, God present to the Word. …Everything was created through him; nothing—not one thing!—came into being without him* (John 1:1-3 MSG).

Although there are some wonderful resources available that will be recommended at the end of this book, the Bible is our ultimate guide and best single source to understanding dreams.

Bible Reading

At this writing, I am reading through my Bible for the 40th time. I began a habit of reading through my Bible once a year when I was young and plan to read at least once a year for the rest of my life. I consider it the best investment I could have made and want to encourage you to make yearly Bible reading a life goal.

There is no other book that establishes godly wisdom, stabilizes your thoughts and actions, and comforts you in every situation and time of life.

> *For we have the living Word of God, which is full of energy, and it pierces more sharply than a two-edged sword. It will even penetrate to the very core of our being where soul and spirit, bone and marrow meet! It interprets and reveals the true thoughts and secret motives of our hearts* (Hebrews 4:12).

Notes

Journaling Your Dreams

Seven Questions

9: Fruits of the Spirit; number of the Holy Spirit; final, or number before ten (complete); faith; the result of the work of Jesus.

June, 1995

In the dream a man came to me and said "I am presenting you with **a new car.**" I was quite thrilled until I saw the car.

I have always been a sports car guy who likes fast cars that handle great and go fast.

The car I was presented in the dream was a 1948-1950s Hudson Hornet of the first uni-body construction of its time. It was dark green color with all the deluxe chrome trim, plush leather interior off-white to beige, large diameter bone-white steering wheel, and column-mounted three-speed shifter with chrome horn rim.

The tires were deluxe white walls with chrome hubcaps and chrome beauty rings on the green wheels, polished wood-trimmed dashboard, all top of the line. The Hornet, as I recall, had a high horsepower straight eight-cylinder flat-head engine.

The man gave me the shiny chrome keys, I got in, started the engine, and began my first drive.

It was powerful but awkward for me. It felt like a boat on water. It did not handle to my liking. But it was now my primary mode of

> transportation with luxury and lots of power.
> —Rich, apostolic leader and teacher

Note the amazing details in this dream. Rich recorded the interior and exterior colors, fabric, and materials used and even described how he *felt* driving the car. He described the year, make, and model; the vehicle's history; and we can even find out what was happening in church history at that time. There are lots of details and they provide value in the interpretation.

Here are some helpful tips and thoughts when writing the dream story.

Journaling: The Seven Questions

Who, what, when, where, why, how did I feel, and how many?

When journaling a dream, it is important to write what you literally saw in the dream, but when interpreting it is important to look at the dream through Jesus's eyes and His thoughts.

Who

A *name definition*, *position*, *occupation*, or *relationship* of a person in your dream will probably *represent* something significant in a dream.

When a *friend or acquaintance* plays a prominent role in a dream, it is easy to assume the dream is about this person. Refuse to jump to this conclusion before taking the following steps. Remember, because you had the dream it is probably about *you and your life*.

Make it a habit to step back from defining your dream by *what you know* about the other person represented in the dream. Instead, look for other meaning behind what this person *represents* to you and how that affects the dream interpretation. For example, your best friend may represent Jesus, who truly is your best friend.

- Research the **name meanings** of the people in your dream as this may be important to the message the dream is conveying.

- **Relationships**—mother, father, brother, sister, cousin, friend, etc. Your mother may represent the church or Holy Spirit. Your grandfather may represent generational blessing, ancestors or the past, an inheritance, or a calling.

- **Position or occupation**: Think about the role the person plays and how what they *do* applies to the dream. Examples: a parent may be a *guardian* or *leader*. A pastor may be *Jesus* or a *shepherd*. A favorite teacher may be *Holy Spirit* or one who gives *knowledge/wisdom*. A *doctor* may be one bringing physical or spiritual healing.

- What is *your role* in the dream? Are you the main character, or are you simply observing?

Other characters may include:

- **Animals** or creatures—record how they made you feel or the role they played.

Notes

Notes

- **Bugs** or spiders—what is the bug/spider's value or traits? Do they sting or bite? This may represent words that sting or hurt.

- **Body parts** like a hand, teeth, hair, eyes. Consider what the body part does. *Hair* (covers your head) may represent your *calling* or *anointing*; *eyes* can represent *vision* or *ability to see in the Spirit*; a pair of *glasses* can represent your *vision* or *the calling* on your life; *teeth* may represent *words*.

What are you doing?

In the dream, are you working? At school, learning? What activity are you involved in? Are you in motion, such as flying or running? Are you using some form of transportation like a bicycle, scooter, skateboard, longboard, hoverboard, skates, airplane, boat, car, truck, or bus? These may represent your life calling, a trade, or business. Vehicles may represent a ministry you are in or called to.

Remember: a ministry is not necessarily preaching from a pulpit. A ministry is doing what you love (hobby, career, raising a family) or taking the good news of Jesus to others in the place where Jesus has positioned you.

Your interests are very important to God. The dream above is an example of how much God loves what you love. Your interests will be included in your dreams and may have extreme detail and even information you did not previously know.

Be sure to write down what catches your attention or what is highlighted as it is important for interpretation. Jesus is speaking, using your interests to highlight His thoughts about you.

Jesus is focused on you and the things you love and want to do.

When: Write the date and time you had the dream at the top of your journal page.

Sometimes you'll know specifically that it is morning, afternoon, evening, midnight. The exact time may be shown on a clock and the number may be significant—1:11, 2:22.

- Are the details of the dream bright and sunny or dark and dismal?

- Is the dream in color, in black and white, or grayscale?

- Is your dream happening during a storm or other noticeable event?

Where is the dream taking place?

Each location can have a significant meaning and its own important role in interpretation.

- What is the location—a town, city, country, building, park?

- Are you in your home or someone else's?

- Are you in a specific part of your house—bathroom, kitchen, upstairs, basement, bedroom, garage?

- Is this place familiar or strange?

- Is there a body of water like a swimming pool, river, lake, ocean, etc.?

Notes

How do you feel in the dream?

How you wake up **feeling** during and after the dream is important. Emotions like happiness, sadness, anger, fear, disgust, confidence, peace, and boldness all show up in dreams and are important to note.

It is also important that you record the **intensity** of the emotion. For example, "In my dream, the lion was roaring very loud, then he turned and roared right in my face! I woke, and my heart was pounding!"

You may also feel emotions that seem **out of place**: "Although the lion was terrifying, I was not afraid and actually felt boldness. I knew he was my best friend. He loved and cared for me with the most intense love I've ever felt. I woke feeling as if he were right beside me and he was giving me strength."

Remember: Jesus is the Lion of Judah and He may appear in your dream as a lion.

You may have **discernment** of good or evil from how you feel in a dream. Snakes or skunks may be a signal of something evil, or a bright sunny day, a playful puppy, or a person who doesn't stop smiling may be a signal of something very good.

Jesus is the happiest person you'll ever meet. Sometimes He or an angel will appear in your dream as a very happy person. If He appears as a lion, you'll know He is good and not going to harm you.

How many and what color?

- In the dream, were there numbers that were highlighted or repeated?

- Is this one dream or a series of two or three dreams that all seem connected?

- Were you shown a formula, an equation, or a list of numbers?

For example, Einstein was shown the formula for his Theory of Relativity in a series of 18 dreams.

The more you keep record of your dreams, the more you'll begin to recognize the elements of your dream that repeat.

It can be tempting to rest on one interpretation or definition for a metaphor. Guard against this and be ready to hear God's creative and unique thoughts about you.

Meanings may change because of the context of the dream. For instance, in one dream the Lion may represent Jesus, and in another dream a lion may turn up as a destructive force and does not have the characteristics of Jesus. The context of the dream is vital!

As you mature, your perspective changes and metaphors can begin to represent different things. *Dream interpretation is fun because you'll soon realize that you have a unique language that is just between you and Jesus.*

Interpretation of the Vehicle Dream

This dream was related to Rich's life and ministry calling.

- **New car**: a new life work, which was awkward at first, not easily handled.

- **1948-1950s**: the time of the healing and deliverance revival. This represented, for Rich, a new type of life work and ministry.

- **Hudson**: In the 1800s, Hudson Taylor was young and he became a prototype evangelist/missionary to China. Hudson used his talent in medicine to spread the gospel and pour his life into the Chinese people. In a similar way, Rich was learning his life assignment was similar to Hudson's.

- **Top of the line**: God provides him with the best equipment inside and out.

- **Uni-body construction**: Rich's heart is to see and equip the body of Christ in the *unity of the body* and the bond of peace (see Eph. 4:3).

- **High horsepower engine**: this represents powerful ministry and the ability and help to do whatever Jesus asks.

All of this was relevant to Rich and his life work. He has even been called to a foreign nation to help equip and bring unity to the body of Christ. This dream began to make sense as he looked at the details.

What is the value of your soul to God? Could your worth be defined by an amount of money? God doesn't abandon or forget even the small sparrow he has made. How then could he forget or abandon you? What about the seemingly minor issues of your life? Do they matter to God? Of course they do! So you never need to worry, for you are more valuable to God than anything else in this world (Luke 12:6-7).

10

Practical Journaling

10: Complete, full.

In my dream I was at Fire Camp. We were sitting down to listen to what Stephanie was saying. I wanted a better spot, so I got up to move forward with one or two other girls, but they started playing instead of listening. I wasn't sure where to sit. I noticed another girl **drinking Coca Cola.** I decided to go over there and drink some, too.

—HANNAH, age 8

Practical Journaling

When I was young, I had a journal but I felt that I did not have very important things to say, so I stopped writing in it. This is not so with my dream journal. I write down my dreams because I know Jesus is speaking to me and it is very important to hear the message He is relaying.

Your dream journal can be one of your favorite books.

When taking time to re-read dreams, you'll find it's surprising how many of the dreams have come true. The patterns and common themes will give you understanding of how Jesus is speaking specifically to you.

Notes

You are never too young or too old for Jesus to speak to you.

Always be listening.

Practical Tips for Journaling

1. Find a notebook that is used only for journaling dreams and visions. A plain old notebook will work or you can purchase a notebook or journal that is special to you. Remember, you will probably want to keep this for a very long time.

2. Keep the journal and a pen beside your bed.

3. Write the dream as soon as possible. If you are awakened by a dream, even in the middle of the night, that is the time to write it down. It is risky to tell yourself you'll remember the dream in the morning. Dreams are quickly lost and when you wake you may have already forgotten the dream story. Recording your dreams takes some discipline, but you will be rewarded by the practice.

My heart is on fire, boiling over with passion. Bubbling up within me are these beautiful lyrics as a lovely poem to be sung for the King. Like a river bursting its banks, I'm overflowing with words, spilling out into this sacred story (Psalm 45:1).

What about a digital voice recorder?

This works as well and is effective particularly if you dream a song, tune, rhythm, or other sound present in your dream. However, keeping a written copy is still important so that the dream is not lost if your device/recording becomes unavailable.

Keep your recording device handy. Make sure you can turn it on when sleepy and speak the dream clearly so you don't miss details. Recordings can be quite funny to hear in the morning.

What should I write down?

Write down the date of the dream and the approximate time you dreamed it. For instance, you may have a vague idea of the time—before midnight, after midnight, or around 4:00 A.M.

There are other times you'll remember exactly what time you woke from the dream because of the pattern of the numbers on the clock (such as 1:11, 3:16, 4:44, etc.).

What details are important?

Whatever stands out, is highlighted, or is impressed in your memory is worth writing down.

- Colors

- Numbers

- Is the dream dark or light?

- The story in the dream

- How did you feel in the dream?

Can I draw the dream?

Yes! Some dreams are best drawn or simply explained with lots of color or shapes.

Do I need to write the dream perfectly?

No, write the dream without concern for grammar or punctuation. The main goal is to get all the details of the dream written.

Notes

After writing the dream, ask Jesus for the interpretation.

You may already understand what the dream is, or you may have no idea. Write what you have, always asking Holy Spirit for more understanding.

A trusted friend can be a key for understanding your dream.

When you tell the dream to a friend, simply saying the dream out loud may help you understand the dream. When stumped by a dream, I will call a trusted friend, repeat the dream, and almost immediately understand what the dream is saying. Your friend may also have insight you would not have thought of.

It is also possible that the dream may actually come true. An event may happen soon after you have the dream and you'll realize this event is what the dream was about.

Remember: If the interpretation connects to your understanding of the dream or is confirmed in your heart, you've correctly interpreted the dream. The interpretation usually brings a confident feeling of understanding. If you have any hesitation that you have the interpretation correct, wait until you learn more.

Dream Interpretation

Hannah was learning how to listen to Holy Spirit at Fire Camp. She had a choice to make—do I go with the ones who are "playing church," or do I move forward and learn to participate with the Holy Spirit? *Coca Cola* represents the effervescent move of the Holy Spirit, and this is what Hannah chose.

11

Dedicating Sleep to God

11: This number can signal disorder, change, or transition; life changes may seem uncertain until you are able to settle in the new situation; transition is good, even when painful, because you are on the way to 12, God's perfect rule in your life.

It is no accident that this chapter is the 11th chapter. Just like the definition for the number 11 above, before you are good at dream interpretation your dreams may be difficult to understand and the process of learning may get a bit frustrating. It takes an investment of time to become good at anything—an instrument, sports, etc. Dream interpretation is no different. If you are willing to dive into the learning process, the return on this investment is well worth the cost.

Remember: You are in the process of becoming an excellent interpreter of dreams. This is a lifelong practice.

What to Do When You Forget a Dream

Ask God to help you remember. A situation in the day may trigger the memory of what you dreamed. If not, pray that the dream will be repeated.

> I had forgotten to write down my dream first thing after waking. I was disappointed in my own forgetfulness but mostly regretted missing the message of the dream. I asked God to give me another opportunity to see the dream. That night, I dreamed the exact same dream again.
> —STEPH

Why is it important to write down my dreams?

Have you ever awakened to realize the memory of your dream is quickly slipping away? Whether you have dreamed for a long time or are new to this, it takes effort to get into the habit of documenting the dream as soon as you receive it.

1. **Dreams are quickly lost.** Memories fade, perceptions of the dream can change, and details can be forgotten. It is very difficult to recover a dream once it is lost.

2. **Honor.** What we honor, we grow to be like. When we ask God to speak to us, it is important to journal the dreams He gives us. This builds honor in our heart toward God. When we honor what God has given, we open up the possibility of receiving more.

3. **Dream History.** When you write down dreams, it makes it possible to review what

you were shown over long periods of time. This builds understanding for interpretation. It is fun to find patterns, repeating stories, or scenarios in your dreams, and it gives understanding to your personal dream language.

No More Alarms

Many years ago, I began to ask Holy Spirit to wake me up in the morning. Since then, I've grown accustomed to no alarm, and I trust Holy Spirit and my body to wake easily in the morning.

If you are in a dream when it is time to wake, a loud noise may make you forget what you are seeing. Dreams are more easily remembered if you repeat details of what you've just seen as you stir yourself to wakefulness.

How to Wake Naturally

Practice this when waking at a certain time is not too important—on a weekend or when you know someone else will wake you if needed.

Before going to sleep, remind your body that you need to wake without an alarm at this specific time. For instance: "I need to wake up at 7:00 A.M.; please help me, Holy Spirit." This is a bit funny, but I say this out loud to myself because I want my body, soul (mind, *will*, and emotions), and spirit to hear it.

Once you have started practicing this, as you transition to learning to wake on time for school or a job, set an alarm five minutes *past the time* you must wake up. This gives you an opportunity to wake naturally, but provides a safety net in case you struggle to wake up.

Remember to turn off the sound on all electronics (cell phones, computers) so that you will sleep deeply and your dreams will not be interrupted through the night. You do

Notes

not want a text message in the middle of the night to interrupt your dream message from God!

Finally, dedicate your times of rest to the Lord. Thank Jesus in advance for any dreams He wants to give you. Now, sleep well and dream.

It is quite surprising the first couple of times you wake naturally, and it feels wonderful when it becomes a useful habit. I promise you'll never miss being jolted awake by an alarm. When Holy Spirit gently awakens you, it brings peace and happiness to your morning, and if you've dreamed you'll be able to wake thinking about your dream. This is just one more way to experience how Jesus loves to be involved in every detail of your life.

> So don't worry. For your Father cares deeply about even the smallest detail of your life (Matthew 10:30-31).

Jesus loves invitations, so before falling asleep:

- Dedicate your time of sleep to the Lord and ask for good sleep.

- Talk to Him as you fall asleep, telling Him how important your dreams are to you and that you want to remember your dreams and write them down.

- Ask God to speak to you in your dreams.

God loves it when we repeat His Word to Him and when we speak truth to ourselves. He loves to answer our prayers, and we honor Him when we invite Him to speak to us.

Don't give up if understanding dreams is difficult at first. Just as you practice music, sports, math, or any other skill you want to excel in, learning to interpret your dreams takes practice, time, and relationship with God.

> If you make history with God, He'll make history through you.
> —BILL JOHNSON, pastor of Bethel Church, Redding, CA

Notes

Dreams Created by God

We have dual citizenship: we are citizens of our own country and we are citizens of Heaven. We need to use our heavenly rights, knowing and exercising our heavenly citizenship. Using this heavenly citizenship, we can ask, "Is it lawful for you (enemy) to attack a son of God, a citizen of Heaven?" Speak, using the Name of Jesus. This brings alarm and terror to the enemy.

—Excerpted from *God's Prophetic Symbolism in Everyday Life* by ADAM F. THOMPSON and ADRIAN BEALE

12

Where Do Dreams Originate?

12: The number of God's perfect government; 12 months in a year, 12 hours in a day, 12 sons of Jacob, 12 apostles. Many times I see this number when God is organizing or aligning my life according to His will.

For through the Son everything was created, both in the heavenly realm and on the earth, all that is seen and all that is unseen. Every seat of power, realm of government, principality, and authority— it was all created through him and for his purpose! He existed before anything was made, and now everything finds completion in him (Colossians 1:16-17).

Dreaming Originates with God

The scripture above is from the ancient book of dreams, God's Word. There is no other book like this one. It is the complete book of wisdom for understanding the spirit realm.

Notes

God alone is creative and all wisdom, knowledge, and creativity comes from Him. We also know that the only way to get true interpretation is from God and His Word.

Young people have related to me how they've been told by important people in their lives that their dreams are from the enemy. No one wants to dream if they know the enemy is going to speak to them. But Scripture tells us that dreams and interpretation originate with God alone.

Can the enemy create a dream?

If so, wouldn't I have to go to the enemy or a psychic for the interpretation?

The answer to both questions is a resounding "*No!*"

The enemy, other external factors, or our own soul can influence, take over, or twist our dreams, but let's always begin with searching out *God's hand first* in the creation of a dream.

> *The God who made the world and everything in it...He makes the creatures; the creatures don't make him. ...He doesn't play hide-and-seek with us. He's not remote; he's near. We live and move in him, can't get away from him!* (Acts 17:24-29 MSG)

Remember: God is the author and originator of dreams.

Note: Of the hundreds of scary dreams we've heard, it is hard to identify a single dream *created* by the enemy. Rather, the dream has been given so that the enemy's evil plan will be fully exposed. The enemy's plans are scary. Uncovering his evil is not fun to see. A scary dream is allowed so that you may tap into God's brilliant strategy to defeat and fully destroy the works of the enemy in your life.

> The enemy steals, counterfeits, imitates, trespasses, and influences; however, it is impossible for him to create anything.

You come and so scare me with nightmares and frighten me with ghosts [or visions] (Job 7:14 MSG).

> *Oh, the overwhelming, never-*
> *ending, reckless love of God*
> *It chases me down, fights 'til I'm*
> *found, leaves the ninety-nine*
> *I couldn't earn it, and I don't deserve*
> *it, still, You give Yourself away*
> *Oh, the overwhelming, never-end-*
> *ing, reckless love of God.*

—"Reckless Love" by Cory Asbury[3]

Notes

13

God Is Motivated to Expose the Enemy!

13: **Although there are negative meanings to this number, Jesus redeems everything!**

Hashem, the Hebrew word for "the Name (God)," has the numerical value of 13. This is true for the Hebrew word for love (ahava), as well. When we love God, we join with Him and love who He is and what He created. Thirteen is fully expressed in the numerical value of His Name and His love. Thirteen is God's number. It implies bonding many into one. God loves being associated with 13, and if you were born on this day you can know that His Name and His love is expressed in the value of this number. You are deeply loved by Him.

The one who doesn't love has yet to know God, for God [Hashem] is love [ahava] (1 John 4:8).

I remember being in my crib; I was about two and a half or three years old. At this time, my parents did not know God. I would wake from dreaming that clowns were in my room. I could see red eyes behind their masks. I was terrified.

—BRENDAN, 10

Have you ever turned on a light and seen bugs scurry for a hiding place? When you shine a very bright light on darkness, you expose what is hiding there.

God has your very best in mind. He sees when the enemy is trying to cause trouble and does all He can to expose or turn a very strong light on the enemy's plans.

Affected by Environment

In Brendan's story above, he was innocently picking up on what was being allowed to enter his home or environment. A *door* or *gate* on our property is a signal to ask for permission to enter onto that property. If we leave the front door open to our house, anything or anyone can walk through it.

We are most aware of the enemy's presence when we are very young because we've not learned to "turn off" spiritual receptiveness. In the Spirit realm, when we do not purposefully close the enemy's spiritual entry points (doors or gates), he will attempt to enter. He does not knock on the door. He trespasses (see John 10:1,10). We have God's Word and His authority to purposefully shut the spiritual door or gate and stop the enemy from entering.

Some would say Brendan's experience is *from the enemy*. The enemy was definitely working to bring fear and destruction, but more importantly God was working to expose the plan of the enemy using Brendan's sharp spiritual perception. The enemy wanted to trap Brendan in a mindset of fear. God in His deep love for Brendan and his family was working to expose every work of the enemy.

When Brendan's mother turned to God for help, they learned how the enemy was gaining entry into their lives and how to disable his entrance into their home. Immediately, the scary dreams and experiences stopped.

> **KEY:** There is not a formula to use when learning how Jesus will deal with the enemy. Instead, we close the door to the enemy by relationship with God, who is the ruler of the spirit realm. When we ask, He will teach us to use the authority in His Word.

Here is a framework of prayer that you may use and adapt to your own situation:

> *Father, I am Your child. Thank You for helping me see if there is an opening that allows the enemy entrance in my dreams. In the Name of Jesus, I command the enemy to **leave** me, my room, and my home. I am a child of the Most High God; my life, my stuff, and my heart belong to Jesus. Thank You, Jesus, for exposing the enemy! I refuse to participate with the spirit of fear, but instead I will boldly call upon You, Father, for You stand with me. You have given me the spirit of **love, power,** and a **sound mind**. I ask You, Jesus, to deal with the enemy on my behalf as the Righteous One who died for me. Thank You for giving me sweet sleep and wonderful dreams because I am Your beloved one. In Jesus's Name.*

> *For God did not give us a spirit of timidity or cowardice or fear, but [He has given us a spirit] of power and of love and of sound judgment and personal discipline [abilities*

that result in a calm, well-balanced mind and self-control] (2 Timothy 1:7 AMP).

Notes

14

Who Are My Dreams About?

14 (7+7): **Double measure of spiritual perfection, deliverance, and liberty.**

I was in West Africa and a young boy, about nine years old, had this dream (interpretation below):

> I dreamed I ended up underneath a very large truck. The driver of the truck pulled me from underneath the truck and set me up on my feet. My mother came and retrieved me.

Who Are My Dreams About?

You!

Most of your dreams are about your own circumstances, people you know, and things familiar to you. When you have a dream, the first assumption you can make is "because I dreamed it, it is about me."

Jesus is always talking. He has great things to say and He wants to talk to you, about you. He is not giving you a story at night simply for your entertainment. He has something important to speak into your life.

A dream is like a parable or a short story.

Usually a dream will be a story with details that are familiar to you. It is intended to captivate your attention and curiosity. Once you are interested in the dream, God's Spirit will cause you to want to figure out the meaning of the dream. This is why a dream will bug you all day or you will be reminded of details of the dream that day or even repeat the dream the next night.

God is inviting you to pursue Him.

He wants you to engage in the dream story that will help you see what is in your own heart. When you search out the correct interpretation, you will get a clearer perspective of your own heart without relying on your own reasoning, logic, or intellect.

In other words, when I try to consider a problem in my life, I may come to my own conclusions instead of hearing God's wisdom on the subject. Dreams break through the barriers so that we can hear God's answer.

When you hear directly from God in a dream, you know He has your best interests in mind. Your life is priceless to Him and He is cheering you on and encouraging you to learn from Him. His intentions and thoughts toward you are always the best!

If my dreams truly are from God, how does He know so much about me?

God created you and knows every detail about you. What if your dreams were meant to help you fulfill a unique purpose in life? What if God gave you a dream that carried an invention that could help many people? Would you value your dreams more if you knew this?

> *The way you counsel and correct me makes me praise you more, for your whispers in the night give me wisdom, showing me what to do next* (Psalm 16:7).

Dream Interpretation

The boy in the dream above, ended up underneath a very *large truck*. (He found himself under the influence of a large ministry.) *The driver* of the truck pulled him from underneath the truck and *set him up on his feet*. (Jesus is the driver of the ministry—He set him upright with knowledge of His love and on a good path.) *The boy's mother came* and retrieved him. (The local church body came to help him grow in his life with God.)

Always Look for the Good Word from God

It is interesting how many times we automatically assume a dream is negative. We judge ourselves harshly and believe that God does the same. We may say we believe that God is good, but in reality we fear that God is angry with us. Remember, you are His beloved child. You are the one He is relentlessly pursuing.

When a dream seems negative, wait to interpret the dream until you remember how deeply you are loved by God.

A true friend tells the truth and keeps you from hurting yourself or others. A true friend rescues you from danger. A true friend counsels you in how to succeed in real-life situations and circumstances.

God is working for your success! He is not angry at you. He is your very best friend.

> *Before I shaped you in the womb, I knew all about you. Before you saw the light of day, I had holy plans for you* (Jeremiah 1:5 MSG).

> *For you bring me a **continual revelation** of resurrection life, **the path to the bliss** [extreme joy] that brings me face-to-face with you* (God) (Psalm 16:11).

What Has Stopped Me from Dreaming?

15 (10 + 5): **Complete + grace—acts of divine grace.**

"I never dream." "I do not remember my dreams." "God does not speak to me in dreams."

These statements are examples of "negative agreements" or "negative declarations" that should not be said about yourself. Ask Jesus to forgive you and help you dream and remember your dreams.

What should I do when it seems I'm not dreaming?

There are several things you can do to become more active in receiving a dream.

When you wake, **journal** everything you remember or what you are thinking about when you wake. You may be surprised to find that you are dreaming, you just were not paying attention to or recalling it. It may take practice to begin remembering your dreams.

Record pictures or impressions you have, whether they happen when awake or asleep—even daydreams. Remember, what you honor increases in your life.

Journal the Bible: Choose a scripture or a book of the Bible and write it out in your journal. Make notes of the principles and thoughts that impact you. A great place to start is the book of Proverbs. God's Word becomes alive to you when you write it down, speak it out loud, sing it, or repeat even one verse over and over.

Sing or repeat God's Word out loud. Actively speaking the Word from memory or reading the Word out loud and listening to the Word opens up your heart to hear revelation from God.

Healthy use of electronics: Science is finding that electronic devices like smartphones, tablets, computers, and gaming devices actually block your ability to get restful sleep. The bright screens delay the brain's ability to produce melatonin, the hormone that induces sleep. It is healthy to turn off the device screens at least 30 minutes before bed and keep them at least five feet away from your bed.

Read a paper book before sleeping. Studies are finding that reading a book printed on paper is heathy for your eyes and brain.

Dedicate times of sleep to the Lord. Ask God to speak to you in dreams and help you to remember your dreams before you fall asleep.

Is there anything that keeps me from dreaming?

1. **Refusing God's voice** and His willingness to speak to you. There are some individuals, even religious people, who refuse to believe that God speaks to them. They reject all incoming forms of communication (dreams, visions, pictures, impressions, etc.) as being from God.

What to do: Search your heart. If needed, ask God to forgive you for rejecting His methods of communication.

Notes

2. **Giving credit to the enemy** for dreams. Be careful to give credit to God for the way He communicates to you. Religious people accused Jesus of working miracles by using satan's power. The enemy loves to put his twist on everything, even trying to take the credit for miracles God has done.

What to do: If in the past you or someone you trusted attributed your dreams to the enemy, ask God to teach you to hear from Him by whatever method He chooses to use. From this time on, ask Jesus what He wants to say to you, listen to His voice, and refuse to give credit to any other source.

3. **Refusing to forgive others**. We all sin; we all have hurt someone unknowingly, accidentally, or (sadly) on purpose. When we refuse to forgive others, it *will block our communication with God* (see Mark 11:25).

What to do: Forgive others and walk in love.

Forgiveness is for our benefit. When we forgive others for wrongdoing toward us, we release the person who has wronged us from any judgement we may have made against them. This allows God to deal with this person directly in the perfect and loving way that only He can.

Forgiveness allows healing to begin to take place in our own heart, thus opening up our ability to hear from God. If you are around a person who is verbally or physically harsh, ask Jesus for His answer to this problem.

Jesus will help you, simply ask. Jesus always hears you when you call to Him. He will give you strength until change happens. Ask Him for His solution. You can be confident that one day, God will set the record straight on all wrongdoing.

4. **Wrong choices** we make directly affect our ability to hear from God.

Notes

What to do: In Psalm 139:24, David said, *"See if there is any path of pain I'm walking on, and lead me back to your glorious, everlasting ways—the path that brings me back to you."* Run to Jesus and into His love. Ask Him to restart your ability to hear from Him. Also read Exodus 20:3-17.

5. **Looking to any other source** or taking a substance in order to have a dream. If you want to dream, simply go to Jesus, the brilliant creator of dreams.

Finally, have a thankful heart regardless of whether you dream or not. Here is an example of how you can pray:

> *I'm so thankful for You, Jesus. I know You are thinking good thoughts about me all the time. If You choose to give me a dream, I am blessed. If You choose to be silent as I sleep, I am blessed. I love how You speak to me and how you created me with the ability to hear Your thoughts. Your willingness to give me wisdom, knowledge, and revelation makes my heart strong and keeps me from fear and doubt. Turn my pillow into a ladder, like you did for Jacob, may I see Your glory when I sleep. Thank You for including me in Your dreams. I dedicate this time of sleep to You. Thank You, Jesus, for who You are and for how You love and take such good care of me.*

> *Taking one of the stones of the place, he put it under his head and lay down there [to sleep]. He dreamed that there was a ladder (stairway) placed on the earth, and the top of it reached [out of sight] toward heaven; and [he saw] the angels of God ascending and descending on it [going to and from heaven]* (Genesis 28:11-12 AMP).

Dreaming 101

Is Dreaming Good for Me?

16: God pouring out His love (John 3:16).

> After working for three days without sleep, Dmitri Mendeleev decided to rest. He immediately fell into a deep sleep and dreamed about arranging chemical elements. This dream changed modern chemistry forever. He said, "I saw in a dream a table where all the elements fell into place as required. Upon awakening, I immediately wrote the table down on a piece of paper...only in one place did a correction later seem necessary."
>
> —DMITRI MENDELEEV telling the story of how he formatted the original Periodic Table of the Elements

Dreaming is good and necessary for your brain like food and water is necessary for your body. Your body must have sleep so that your brain, organs, and heart will continue to work properly. Dreams are equally important to your emotional health. When you lack good sleep, you may feel more stressed, frustrated, or sad. Good sleep helps you feel hopeful and happy and brings motivation to accomplish projects.

Remember: Your dreams bring health to your physical body. Have you ever had a computer stop working or a cell phone start flashing or refusing to work properly? The first step to fix a tech issue is to restart or reboot the device.

In a similar way, when you sleep your body sends a new batch of substances to your brain that reboot your ability to concentrate, make decisions, recall information, and create. This nightly brain refresh even boosts your ability to fight off sickness or to recover from injury.

No time is wasted while you sleep.

Scientists believe that you may actually dream about two hours out of eight hours of sleep. But the amazing thing is the other hours of sleep may be used in other forms of healthy dreamlike thought. It is true, we are fearfully and wonderfully made!

> *You will sleep like a baby, safe and sound—your rest will be sweet and secure. …God is your confidence in times of crisis, keeping your heart at rest in every situation* (Proverbs 3:24,26).

> *Don't you know he enjoys giving rest to those he loves?* (Psalm 127:2 MSG)

17

Pizza Dreams

17: Victory; walking with God; complete rest.

> I had a "pizza dream" last night! It was the craziest dream ever and I'm sure it doesn't mean anything.
>
> —Commonly heard from those who dream

Embarrassingly Crazy and Impossible Dreams

Dreams may trigger all sorts of reactions—laughter, tears, embarrassment, outrage, or even being completely repulsed by what you've just seen. Typically, these odd dreams are written it off as "pizza dreams." However, because you witnessed an impossible situation in the dream, you may stumble onto an excellent bit of wisdom that will apply to your life.

"Pizza Dreams" Are Valuable

These dreams may seem impossible dreams to interpret, but I want to encourage you to ask Holy Spirit and search out the meaning of every dream you are blessed to receive.

Notes

> *This is the wildest dream I've ever had and is pretty embarrassing! I was in an outhouse. I was **not** happy to be in there. Then I saw a white snake with red stripes and red eyes that I had left in the toilet. The snake was dead and I was grossed out.*
> —HEATHER, age 15

Interpretation

An **outhouse** or **bathroom** is where we go to get rid of stuff our body is finished with. It can also represent repentance or confession.

A **white snake** can represent a lie. In this dream, the snake is white. A "white lie" is considered a harmless lie. A white lie can be more dangerous than an obvious lie because it hides behind partial truth.

The **red stripes and red eyes** on this snake represent a poisonous snake/lie, and thankfully, in the dream, it is now dead. The dreamer had discarded the snake/lie in the toilet by refusing to believe the lie any more. The lie itself is dead and being flushed out of her life because of confession and forgiveness. The dream is giving the dreamer an opportunity to participate in the solution.

The **"grossed out"** emotion connected to the dream signals the dreamer is being taught to give no more power to this lie or allow it to influence her thoughts or actions. When we realize we've been lied to or have participated in a lie, it can be repulsive to us and can give us resolve and strength to never participate with any part of lying again.

In a dream, when we find ourselves in crazy or impossible circumstances, it may be an excellent opportunity to learn something that has been hidden from our understanding. At first, the above dream may seem negative, but the message is very positive and helpful to Heather.

Since we are now joined to Christ, we have been given the treasures of redemption by his blood—the total cancellation of our sins—all because of the cascading riches of his grace. This superabundant grace is already powerfully working in us, releasing within us all forms of wisdom and practical understanding (Ephesians 1:7-8).

Remember: An embarrassing, offensive, impossible, or crazy story line in a pizza dream may be the key to helping you remember the dream.

Sweet Dreams and Cheese

There may be some truth to the premise that cheese makes you more able to receive and remember a dream. A study conducted in 2005 by the British Cheese Board found that when eating cheese before sleep, 67 percent of participants were able to remember and record their dreams, enjoy pleasant sleep, and none reported having nightmares.

Although this study may be valid, there is no need to eat, drink, or take any other substance to dream. God, the sovereign Creator of dreams, will give you the right dream at the right time. Rest in Him; you are His beloved one—sleep well and dream.

Notes

18

Emotionally Charged Dreams

18 (10 + 8): Complete + new beginning—completely putting off the old life before Jesus.

LIFE and the number 18: the Hebrew letters that spell "chai," or "life," add up to 18.

I was in a very large arena that also seemed like a train station with a stage. Thousands of people were passing through this place; most people were not in a hurry. I briefly looked around at people milling around on this huge stage, seemingly without purpose or direction. I did not recognize anyone. On one side of the stage was a massive fire. The fire had no beginning or end—no top or bottom. The curtain of fire seemed like it reached into the heavens and pressed right up against this stage on earth, then continued below the earth. The fire seemed to burn without fuel. It was the hottest, brightest fire I've ever seen and was the color and intensity of the sun. The opposite end of the stage was darkness. I walked toward a guard who was standing holding his AK-47. I already knew what he was going to tell me—I had a choice of denying Jesus or running into the fire. Without exchanging words, asking questions, or processing the decision, I

> ran as hard and as fast as I could toward the fire. I
> woke covered in sweat and shaking.

When I first woke from this dream, I thought I it was a nightmare! I was completely covered with sweat, shaking, and wondering if this was going to happen to me in reality.

I wrote down the dream and did not go back to it until after enough time had passed that I was no longer emotionally stirred by the dream. Had I interpreted the dream immediately, the emotion attached to the dream may have flavored the interpretation *negatively*. I could have discarded the dream, thinking the enemy was involved in some way.

How long do you wait to interpret a dream that is very emotional?

It is wise put an emotionally stirring dream *interpretation* on hold for several hours, a full day, or longer if the dream is highly emotional. If I repeat the dream to friends, the dream will become clearer and less tied to emotion.

As you practice, you'll begin to know how long to wait to settle on an interpretation for an emotional dream.

The intense emotion of the dream made the dream stick in my memory. I had this dream when I was approximately 23 years old. God allowed me to experience intense emotion, which was even accompanied by a physical reaction. Without this, I may have forgotten the dream. Although I've had many dreams since, this dream impacted my life and is seared into my memory forever.

Do I need to write down what I feel in the dream?

Yes! We were created to experience life. God made our minds and bodies able to feel joy, sadness, and fear as a way to process what is happening around us. In our dreams, we can experience emotion just like when we are awake.

What to Do with an Emotionally Charged Dream

When you have a dream that leaves you angry, sad, puzzled, or afraid, assume that God has allowed this for a reason and write the dream down, noting your emotional reaction to the dream.

Emotions are very strong, and if we allow them too much influence, they will lead us off track. When writing the dream, be careful to not interpret the dream as you write it down. Intense feelings can lead you to add something to the dream that is not there.

Before interpreting an emotional dream, take a break.

After you've journaled the dream, put it away. Intense emotion makes your heart vulnerable and can easily lead you into a negative mindset. Remember:

> God has not given us a spirit of fear, but
> of **power** and of **love** and of a **sound mind**
> (2 Timothy 1:7 NKJV).

I will actually say this verse over myself to keep from being tempted to interpret or be negative to what I've seen while still connected to emotion from a dream. Instead, I ask God for His thoughts and interpretation at the right time.

When emotion from the dream is quiet, then it is time to ask for interpretation.

We want to interpret our dreams with a *sound mind* and with God's heart as our guide. God has the absolute best plans for you and is always thinking good thoughts toward you. He is planning your success, your future, and is ready to give you strength to make it. He is trying to bring encouragement and spur you on to accomplish greater things than you can imagine. He is the ultimate life coach.

> *For I know the thoughts that I think toward you, says the Lord, thoughts of **peace** and not of evil, to give you a **future** and a **hope*** (Jeremiah 29:11 NKJV).

Notes on Dream Interpretation

In the above dream, although I woke afraid, I was more shocked at the intensity of my willingness to run full force into the fire. In my dream language, this represents running into Jesus and His plan for my life without thought for my own life or safety.

- **The large arena** is a picture of my *life* (Acts 1:4).

- **Train station/platform:** A place of decision, waiting, and preparing for ministry or career (Acts 1:4).

- **Many people:** Many pass through this area quickly, not considering God's plans (Matt. 9:36).

- **Wandering people:** Many are not sure of their direction or do not have a plan (Matt. 9:36).

- **Fire burning without fuel:** This represents God's Presence and running into God's purpose. His glory and plan is the ultimate goal (Deut. 4:24; Exod. 24:17; Song of Sol. 8:6-7).

Notes

- **Darkness at the opposite end of the stage:** No direction, no purpose or plan. Selfish agenda (John 12:46).

- **Darkness:** Absence of Jesus, worldliness (John 8:12).

- **Guard:** A gunman is the enemy himself, who would try to stop us with "bullets," which represent "words and accusation." The good word is Isaiah 54:17—no weapon formed against us will prosper!

- **AK-47:** An automatic assault rifle. Can represent threatening words, accusation, meant to stop destiny (Ps. 64:3; Jer. 9:8).

Strong emotional dreams can convey messages from Heaven that impact our life.

This dream was instrumental in my life. Even though I was weak and fearful in real life, this helped me see myself through Jesus's eyes with His courage to face my circumstances with boldness.

My mind, will, and emotions are willing to say "yes" to whatever assignment God has for me, even if asked to lay down my life.

Additional Dream Interpretation Thoughts

In the dream, I knew the gun the guard was carrying was an AK-47. I have no idea how I knew this, other than Jesus plainly revealed it in the dream. I took the opportunity to research and learn about this type of gun. I researched when the AK-47 was used in history, what was its main function or ability, who invented it, etc.

This may be an exercise in research for my own education or there may be a reason that I need to know what this type of weapon is to interpret this dream—or help others. I've learned it is helpful to take time to study about whatever subject God highlights in a dream.

Dreams can have very detailed and even surprising information included.

God cares about your hobbies and what fascinates you. For instance, an airline pilot may dream exact specifications of an airplane engine, specific mechanical information, airports, wind speeds, or other information related to flying. Because this is his profession and/or hobby, he will better understand what God is saying in the dream. It is similar to having a secret code between you and Jesus.

Jesus always has good things to say!

Jesus can speak to us about any subject known to man and those not yet understood—with astonishing detail. It is fun to learn His language and wisdom and to realize He and His message are always for our good.

Notes

19

Dreams Bring Opportunity for Change

19 (10 + 9):   Complete + fruitfulness; fullness of the Spirit.

I Did Not Like This Dream!

It seemed like I was watching a marathon. Repeatedly, young men were being sent into a maze with instructions to find an unknown person or path. It was some sort of game—they could escape the maze but many times were immediately forced into another maze. The young men willingly participated, but once they started the game it seemed they were pushed into more mazes until exhausted. Some of the young men made it out fine, some got lost in the maze, some were terrorized by the game.

Regardless, it was hard to watch and made me angry at what was happening. It seemed they were in a trap but had been tricked into believing the lie that they were where they wanted to be. I woke from the dream at 1:30 A.M. knowing I was to pray for young people who are being trapped into an industry, system, false religion, or mindset that keeps them bound by lies or false promises. I also prayed that they would find their way out of the maze of lies that keeps them trapped. I looked up Deuteronomy 1:30 (I woke at 1:30 A.M.) which says, *"Do not be terrified, or afraid of them. The Lord your God who goes before you, He shall fight for you"* (Deut. 1:29-30 MEV).

Dreams have the ability to bring change.

A dream can teach us to pray in agreement with Jesus and what is on His heart.

When we dream something that is difficult or makes us angry, in that moment, we are called to agree with Heaven and demand change according to God's Word. When we see someone being treated wrongly, unmercifully, or being trapped by a mindset or even a game, we call upon the God of the universe and ask for His thoughts and His plan for change.

> *Our Father in heaven, reveal who you are. Set the world right; do what's best—as above [in heaven], so below [on earth]. Keep us alive with three square meals. Keep us forgiven with you and forgiving others. Keep us safe from ourselves and the Devil. You're in charge! You can do anything you want! You're ablaze in beauty! Yes. Yes. Yes* (Matthew 6:9-13 MSG).

A dream may give you a prayer assignment from Jesus.

To be really effective in prayer, listen to what Jesus has on His mind. He is always looking for people who live here on earth to pray in agreement with Heaven for God's Kingdom plan and ideas to be established here on earth.

Notes

You are a part of God's Kingdom—to Him your prayer is priceless!

Notes

When we wake from a dream, there is no pressure to think up great-sounding, lofty prayers. We can simply agree with the Father, Son, and Holy Spirit as He accomplishes His word. When we join in with the great 24/7 prayer meeting in Heaven, we are joining with the prayer that Jesus prayed to His Father, *"Your Kingdom come. Your will be done on earth as it is in heaven"* (Matt. 6:10 NKJV).

Here is an example of how you can pray when you wake from an intercession dream:

> *Jesus, this dream frustrated me, scared me, made me angry (etc., tell Him how the dream made you feel). I know You want to bring change, and I agree with Your plan. I ask that You will open eyes and ears of those who do not know they are in a trap. I ask you to give a way of escape to those who are captivated by lies. I agree with You, Your Kingdom come, Your will be done on earth as it is in Heaven. In Jesus's Name.*

This type of dream and the prayer it brings from your heart is a big deal in God's Kingdom. Be one who will say "yes" and agree with what is on Jesus's heart.

It is not always necessary to stay awake and pray for a long time, but it is important to join in with what is important to God's heart and be in agreement with what He is doing 24/7, even as you sleep.

> *He is our hope-promise of a future inheritance which seals us until we have all of redemption's promises and experience complete freedom— all for the supreme glory and honor of God!* (Ephesians 1:14)

Nightmares

For God will never give you the spirit of fear, but the Holy Spirit who gives you mighty power, love, and self-control.

—2 Timothy 1:7

It only takes a spark, remember, to set off a forest fire. A careless or wrongly placed word out of your mouth can do that. By our speech [words] we can ruin the world, turn harmony to chaos, throw mud on a reputation, send the whole world up in smoke and go up in smoke with it, smoke right from the pit of hell.

—James 3:6

Dark Dreams, Nightmares, and Their Purpose

20: **Expectancy; waiting; wisdom; complete (10) x (2) multiplication.**

> *I was standing in line in front of a familiar group of stores. There was a registration table that I had to reach in order to go into the "stores." Then I realized the stores were only storefronts. There was an **amusement park** behind the **storefronts**. The **sky was cloudy and dark** but the rides in the park were compelling. It was my turn to pay, and as I stepped up to the registration table the man who was going to take my money jumped over the table and started beating me up! I was able to get away, but he chased me and attacked me again! This kept repeating and I was afraid!*
>
> *Somehow, I beat him off and escaped. I realized the storefronts were not real and the amusement park was a trap to get me in. woke, shook up, my heart beating fast.*
> —CJ, age 11

This particular dark dream could seem like it came from the enemy; however, the dream actually saved the young man from what could have been an extremely bad choice where he could have suffered serious consequences or injury. This dream was not from the enemy. It was from God.

Remember: The only One who is interested in destroying the works of the enemy is God. The only One who is ready to expose the enemy's plans is God!

Interpretation of this dream alerted CJ to the possibility of danger ahead.

CJ had been able to talk about the dream with his mother when he woke that morning. They had considered the meaning of the dream and realized it was a warning.

The very next day, in real life, CJ was offered a trip to a skate park that sounded like a lot of fun (similar to the amusement park in the dream). CJ knew immediately that the invitation was a "false front" (like the false storefronts) and there may have been the possibility of harm to him. The dream story exposed the enemy's plan, and it was very easy for CJ to decline the invitation because of the details in the dream that brought clarity of the possibility of harmful intentions others may have.

A Nightmare's Purpose

Many of the nightmares that have been recalled to us over the years have overwhelmingly been merciful warnings from God that kept the dreamer from trouble, exposing a trap the enemy had set or offering a path of escape from trouble. A true friend will lovingly tell the truth to keep you from a negative experience. Jesus is the best friend you'll ever have.

Before writing off a dream as from an evil source, remember the true Word from God:

> *In a dream, for instance, a vision at night, when men and women are deep in sleep, fast asleep in their beds—God **opens their ears** and impresses them with **warnings** to **turn them back from something bad they're planning**, from some **reckless choice**, and keep them from an **early grave**, from the river of no return* (Job 33:15-18 MSG).

> *Then You [God] scare me with dreams and terrify me with visions* (Job 7:14 NKJV).

Remember: *God is good, all the time. All the time, God is good!*

21

Umbrella of Protection

21:   Expecting God or serving God (20 + 1); fullness or completion (3 x 7 = 21); the enemy stood in opposition to Daniel for 21 days in Daniel 10:13.

> I was standing in a car-wash bay. There was a deck you could walk out on. This seemed like a "lookout" or observation deck. I was looking at a mountain range and could see Gossamer from the Bugs Bunny cartoons coming after me. Gossamer was huge and looking right at me! My dad was not with me.
> —BRENT, recalling a repeating dream from childhood

[The enemy's plan:] A thief has only one thing in mind—he wants to steal, slaughter, and destroy. [God's plan:] But I have come to give you everything in abundance, more than you expect—life in its fullness until you overflow! (John 10:10)

How do I stop the enemy from having access to my life?

1. Dedicate yourself to Jesus.

2. Break all agreement with the enemy: "I have no agreement with the enemy and refuse to participate with anything that would give him access to my life."

3. Ask Jesus for His love to cover you and surround you for whatever you've seen, heard, or done that would allow the enemy access into your life.

4. Thank Jesus for keeping you in His protection and helping you hear and follow His voice and direction.

Your surroundings do affect your dreams.

It is important to keep your environment in mind as you interpret your dreams. You may be unaware of something that is going on in your home or neighborhood, but God will expose what is happening in a dream.

We can innocently pick up on what someone else is intentionally involved in. We may have no idea that someone close by is actively inviting the enemy into the area where we live and this is causing us to see it in our dreams/visions.

In other words, you may feel like the enemy is trying to terrify you in a dream, when actually God is exposing a problem that resides in your home or community, and this has stirred Him to come to your defense. He may be showing Himself available to intervene.

It is important to consider these questions when looking at your dreams.

- Is God exposing something that I need to know so that I can avoid trouble and stop the enemy?

- Am I giving the enemy an open door or gate into my life?

Notes

Notes

Know whose umbrella you are standing under.

When it is pouring rain, you stand under an umbrella for protection. Similarly, you must choose to stand under only one of two leaders in the spirit realm. Jesus is the One who loves you and will teach you to maneuver the spirit realm with His Word and His Holy Spirit. The other "umbrella" is held by the enemy. *When you choose who you will serve, you stand under that "umbrella" or covering for protection.*

You may say, "I am not going to choose one of these, I'll do my own thing, I'll hold my own umbrella." I know this sounds like an easy way out; however, this is the default choice for allowing the enemy access to your life. This is not a safe place. This is an open door for the enemy to influence your mind, will, and emotions (see Rom. 6:16; 1 Pet. 5:8).

If you love and serve Jesus, you are filled with His Holy Spirit. When you follow Him, you are under His umbrella of protection.

If you are being harassed or held down by evil thoughts, actions, or opportunities, ask Jesus how you stepped out from under His protection. When you turn to Him for forgiveness and direction, He will help you stay completely covered by His umbrella of protection and care.

Dream Interpretation

Car-wash bay: A vehicle can represent you/your life. In this dream, the car wash represented the need for Jesus to wash all sin away from his life.

The deck and lookout: Brent was able to "see" what is happening at a "higher level." God was showing him what was happening in the spirit realm.

Gossamer is a hairy orange monster from the Bugs Bunny cartoon series. He has a rectangular shaped body, two giant tennis shoes, and huge arms that end with claws on his fingers. He is covered in bright red/orange hair.

- The **color orange** in the context of this dream signifies a warning, and because the hair covers his whole body he represents a *strong warning of danger*. Obviously, Gossamer is a "monster," which signals danger.

- The word **gossamer** means a thin type of fragile, transparent material, like sheer gauze or a cobweb. From this we understand that Gossamer, or the enemy he represents, is fragile and able to be defeated (by Jesus).

God is revealing what the enemy has to offer—fear. The monster, Gossamer, is trying to instill fear in Brent and God wants to give Brent the ability to defeat the *spirit of fear* and no longer live under the enemy's influence or power.

The Very Good News

When Brent was 13, he gave his heart to Jesus and the dream that had tormented him never returned. Jesus's love, forgiveness, and covering defeated "Gossamer" and the fear associated with this dream.

> *You will keep in perfect and constant peace the one whose mind is steadfast [that is, committed and focused on You—in both inclination and character], because he trusts and takes refuge in You [with hope and confident expectation]* (Isaiah 26:3 AMP).

Notes

"For I know the plans and thoughts that I have for you," says the Lord, "plans for peace and well-being and not for disaster, to give you a future and a hope" (Jeremiah 29:11 AMP).

22

Lock the Gate

22: Expecting testimony (20 + 2); light; double the meaning of 11 (11 x 2).

> *I had been sound asleep when something slammed its fist down on my nightstand. It yelled, "I'm an angel!" However, it was the most horrifying voice I've ever heard. I woke, shaking and terrified. I told it to leave immediately in Jesus's Name! It has not returned.*
> —JILL, age 16

For God has not given us a spirit of fear, but of power and of love and of a sound mind (2 Timothy 1:7 NKJV).

Eradicating Fear Experiences and Nightmares

When you give your life to God, it is illegal for the enemy to speak to you or torment you in any way. The enemy does not obey the law. He trespasses, he lies, he does not fight fairly or according to our wishes. When the enemy attempts any of these tactics, you must command him to stop in Jesus's Name.

Jesus has given us permission to use His Name, His lifeblood, and His authority as protection against all works of the enemy. Jesus has final say and full power over the enemy, and our agreement with Him and His word is our privilege and access to strong help.

It is important to *honor* Jesus and His instruction and *refuse* to give the enemy any avenue of entry. This is your *choice*.

> *Now you understand that I [Jesus] have imparted to you all my authority to trample over his [satan's] kingdom. You will trample upon every demon before you and overcome every power Satan possesses. Absolutely nothing will be able to harm you as you walk [with Me] in this authority* (Luke 10:19).

Just as you lock the door behind you so a thief cannot get into your home, it is important to check every area, gate, or door of your life so the enemy has no way of entering.

God created us with the ability to pick up on what is happening in the supernatural, good or bad. We were created with brilliant "gates" or doorways so that we can be fully alive and a part of the daily give and take of information in the natural and in the supernatural realm around us. Our gates may include, but are not limited to:

- Your eyes (sight) and ears (hearing)

- Your will and emotions

- Your sense of touch, taste, and smell

- You interests and the knowledge you gain

- Your imagination or what you focus on and spend time with

- Any natural sense God has given you that helps you participate with God and His spirit realm—art, nature, using your natural talents. For instance, some may feel very close to God when playing baseball or sewing, so much so that they learn how to pick up on God's realm and learn to excel in their gifts because they've tapped into Heaven's creativity.

Gate Openers

We can open the gate of Heaven or hell in our life. First, let's look at how we allow opportunity for the enemy to cause trouble.

Much like a thief, the enemy checks to see if we've left a gate open for him. When we hear a lie about ourselves, we can actually begin to live out this lie. We all must remember that our words can wound and ruin a person's life. (Please read James 3:6 at the beginning of this section.)

Let's use stealing as an example.

A young man, Panders, accidentally picked up someone else's backpack at school. Panders returned the backpack but was labeled a thief in the process. The declaration stuck, and the rumor that he was a thief continued. Panders began to focus on and practice stealing and soon he was regularly being called a thief. Panders found it uncanny how easy it became to pick up things that were not his on a regular basis.

What Panders may have not realized is that once you begin to actively participate with sin, like stealing, the enemy spirit realm takes notice and will bring scenarios into your life making it easier to steal. The law of attraction (what you participate in attracts others involved in the same activity) was set in motion and soon he was surrounded by friends who were just as good at stealing as he was.

I presented a scenario here; if there is not an active decision made by Panders to stop participating with the sin of stealing and to disagree with the evil declaration made over his life, he will end up in prison or worse. Many times it is simply our own decisions that cause problems, and the enemy may not have much to do with it. However, when we continue in sin we open the door or gate to the enemy and he takes the opportunity to make the situation worse.

KEY: We cannot blame everything on the enemy. It is important to always ask Holy Spirit to check our heart. Jesus sees every tiny movement away from Him and His protection and love.

The fantastic news is that Jesus has sent Holy Spirit and very strong angels to help us resist the enemy and flee from trouble. It is as simple as asking for help. When we refuse to participate with what the enemy is doing, we close the gate to the enemy and his plans.

Dreams are a fantastic key to discern when a door has been left open to give the enemy access to our lives. God has given us the best tools to keep our eyes open to our own bad plans but also expose the schemes of the enemy. God wants you to know what the enemy is planning against you and will do all He can to fully expose evil.

When a dream has **dark elements** like a dark sky, a dark room, or instead of being in color the dream is in black and white, Jesus wants to bring an issue to your attention so you can deal with it.

The emotion of **fear** may be triggered during a dream, which will ensure your ability to remember this dream.

> **KEY:** When we open the gate to Heaven, all good things of Heaven are set in motion. When the opposite gate is open, all hell is set in motion (see James 3:5-6).

Physical reactions like breathing hard, sweating, or suddenly waking are a part of the normal adrenaline rush you get when in danger. Jesus never gives us a *spirit* of fear, but He allows our human emotions to alert us to this present danger threatening our spiritual and physical life.

If this happens, our agreement and actions are extremely important. Refuse to agree with the spirit of fear; instead, agree with the Spirit of love, power, and sound mind.

Next, talk to Jesus. Typically you'll know exactly what sin you've participated with that brought on this dream or experience. Don't disregard the prompting that is in your own heart. Simply tell Jesus everything and ask for His solution. Look for God's strategy in the dream to defeat the enemy.

Remember: Instead of assuming the enemy is speaking in the dream, *focus on what Jesus is revealing.*

Lock the Gate

1. Ask God to show you how the enemy gained access to your life.

Notes

2. Pray over yourself—ask God for His forgiveness for whatever action opened a door to the enemy and then declare Scripture over your life. God's Word is a powerful weapon against the enemy.

3. Thank God for His forgiveness, protection, and love.

4. Ask Holy Spirit to be a guard at the door of your heart and teach you to make wise choices.

5. Remind yourself whose Kingdom you belong to and ask Holy Spirit to help you participate with His thoughts and plans.

6. Refuse to participate with any temptation or trap that would put you in agreement with the enemy's plans.

7. Refuse to believe any lie from the enemy, including what others may say about you. This is how I process what people say about me. I ask, "Would Jesus say this about me?" I've learned to participate with only what Jesus would say and consider all other information less important.

God means what he says. What he says goes. His powerful Word is sharp as a surgeon's scalpel, cutting through everything, whether doubt or defense, laying us open to listen and obey. Nothing and no one is impervious to God's Word. We can't get away from it—no matter what (Hebrews 4:12-13 MSG).

Discernment

Discernment is learning to evaluate good or evil with the power of the Holy Spirit. The experience at the beginning of this chapter was from an evil spirit. How do I know? I look at how the spirit acted. With practice, it becomes easier to discern whether a spirit is good or evil.

- God's voice may be firm, but He will not yell at you.

- He will never slam or throw things. His Spirit is always gentle.

- God operates with the fruit of the Spirit— love, joy, peace, kindness (see Gal. 5:22).

KEY: When learning to discern whether a spirit is from God or the enemy, pay attention to the *characteristics or actions* of the spirit in question.

Jesus is working for your success. Jesus always has very good things to say about you!

In Jill's dream experience, the enemy wanted to do two things.

1. Cause fear by violently yelling and slamming his fist down

2. Attempt to deceive Jill

He could have truthfully stated that he was a *fallen* angel or a demon, but his true intentions were to cause fear and make Jill believe he was powerful and from God. This could have caused a serious problem, but because Jill had the gift of discernment from the Holy Spirit, the actions and character of this spirit were easily discerned as that of an evil spirit. Jill took proper action, commanding the enemy to leave (in Jesus's Name) and to never return. She also checked her heart, making sure there was no participation with sin, to be sure the enemy would be unable to repeat his charade.

Character of God

- Full of love

- Casts out all fear with perfect love

- Gives you free will

- Sets you free from sin by laying down His own life

- Does all He can, without overstepping your free will, to keep you from the enemy's trap

Character of the enemy

- Full of hate

- Rules with fear and terror

- Wants to take your freedom and keep you in bondage

- Wants to keeps you bound to darkness with fear, lies, sin, and addiction

Prayer

*Father, thank You for giving me a spirit of love, power, and a sound mind. I ask for Your forgiveness for opening any doors to the enemy or giving him a place in my heart. I want to participate with **all** You are doing, Jesus, and I ask You to stop the terror* *that the enemy is trying to trap me with. I am Your child and You surround me with Your Holy Spirit so that there is no place for any other spirit or curse to land. I love how You love me and take care of me. Thank You for good sleep and that I am Your beloved one. I commit my sleep to You, Jesus, and ask You for good dreams.*

Notes

Death and Troubling Dreams

Death Dreams

23: The number two represents a double portion, complete (2 x 10), and three is resurrection. This number reminds us of the abundant, complete love Jesus gives us in His resurrection.

When my grandfather died, he was ready to transition to Heaven, but I was not ready to let him go. I was distraught with grief because all of my life we had been very close. I could not imagine life without him, and I was having difficulty moving forward.

Dream

I was in my room. My grandfather walked in the door and hugged me. He said, "Hannah, don't cry for me anymore. I'm with Jesus and I'm doing exactly what I love to do and I am able to accomplish what I was created for. I'm very happy here!"

This dream/experience completely changed my thoughts about losing my grandfather. I no longer grieve his passing but am very happy he is with Jesus and many of his friends and family. I look forward to seeing him again someday.
—HANNAH, age 18

Declaration

It is a good practice to immediately bring the dream to Jesus and declare His Word, which says:

> *You will not let them kill me, but I will live to tell the world what the Lord has done for me* (Psalm 118:17).
>
> *I shall not die, but live, and declare the works of the Lord* (NKJV).

Transition from this life to our heavenly home is a natural part of life.

Obviously, because you are reading this, you are alive and have not personally experienced physical death yet. Fear of death may overtake us if we have experienced the pain of watching someone we love die.

A death dream may alert us to an impending death. This may be a compassionate opportunity to say what we must say to our loved ones and be intentional with whatever time we have left with them. These dream experiences can begin to prepare us for future loss so that we will not despair but rather find comfort and confidence that God knows the purpose and number of our days. Jesus is available to give us abundant hope and the comfort of Heaven.

My friend Janet had this life-changing experience:

> In real life my precious Shih Tzu (dog), Ginger, had died. Ginger was 15 years old and had been a constant comfort and companion to me through very devastating life circumstances. She had even saved my life by reversing my willingness to completely give up as suicidal thoughts tormented me. I knew there would be no one to love Ginger like

I had, so I chose to live. Now she was gone. I was traumatized and overcome with grief.

Janet's Vision/Dream

> I saw Jesus holding Ginger in His lap. Ginger looked much younger now, completely healthy and very happy! I'm not even sure she was missing me! I realized Jesus was looking at me with the most beautiful eyes I had ever seen. He smiled and as we locked eyes a tangible, unexplainable peace flooded over me. I felt immediately healed from the trauma of Ginger's death. Jesus flooded me with overwhelming **joy** like I had never experienced. I was fully alive in Jesus's Presence. This was the realest moment of my life. I woke laughing, overwhelmed by the love of Jesus and the indescribable joy of Heaven. My perspective of death has forever changed. Instead of grief, I have joy-filled expectation to see Jesus and Ginger someday soon.
> —JANET

This life and transition to life in Heaven is in Jesus's loving hands.

A pastor friend, Carl Hahn, has written of his experiences with Holy Spirit for the past 15 years. He is nearing his own transition to Heaven because he is almost 90 years of age. Carl has had the opportunity to dialogue with Holy Spirit about his own future death. When questioning Holy Spirit if death would be painful or difficult, Holy Spirit revealed to him that death is like breathing out air from your lungs here on earth and breathing your next breath in Heaven. It is that simple.

Notes

Notes

Precious [and of great consequence] in the sight of the Lord is the death of His godly ones [so He watches over them] (Psalm 116:15 AMP).

We will still have a God-built home that no human hands have built, which will last forever in the heavenly realm. We inwardly sigh as we live in these physical "tents," longing to put on a new body for our life in heaven.... God himself is the one who has prepared us for this wonderful destiny. And to confirm this promise, he has given us the Holy Spirit, like an engagement ring, as a guarantee (2 Corinthians 5:1-2,5).

24

Warning Dreams

24: Governmental perfection. There are 24 thrones and elders mentioned in Revelation 4:4.

This is from Melissa, a ministry friend and mother:

After our Wednesday night church service, I got the kids home and tucked them in bed at 8:30. An hour later I was straightening up the house and I heard Molly jump out of her bed and call my name. She said, "Mom, I had a vision of Stephanie and a girl with a ponytail walking in India and a man stops them both and asks them if they know Jesus."

I said, "I'm not sure what that means, but if the Lord showed you something then we should act on it." So we knelt down and prayed for you (Stephanie) and the girl with a ponytail.

I tucked her back in to bed and reassured Molly that God showed her that for a reason. We may never know why, but Jesus knew Molly would respond to the vision.

The vision experience above happened while my missionary friend Nicol and I (Stephanie) were traveling in India. At the time of Molly's vision, Nicol and I happened to be in a place where we could have been in danger. It was comforting to know, after the event, that one of our Fire Camp girls had had the vision and prayed. Molly knew nothing of our travels and had not met Nicol, who commonly wears her hair in a ponytail.

Dreams That Come True

Even very young children can have dreams that come true. If we become upset or fearful because of a dream, we are acting on the premise that God is not good. The opposite is true. God is good and we have the power to speak His truth and goodness into the situation.

Every dream or vision is an opportunity to encounter the goodness of God. Try to see the dream from His eyes and His perspective knowing He has your success in mind.

Melissa set an excellent example in the above vision. Let's be the best at calling out the positive possibilities concerning unsettling dreams/visions and realize this is the moment that Jesus is offering His strategy, goodness, and peace for the situation. We join in the 24/7 prayer meeting that is in progress in Heaven and declare, with Jesus, His very best for every circumstance regardless of what we see or hear in the natural.

Please consider these important steps to follow after having a death or disturbing dream.

- Jesus is all about keeping you in peace and helping you stabilize in His love. You can trust Jesus and His wisdom in giving you the dream. Ask Him to comfort your heart and help you understand His purpose and plan.

- *Refuse* to agree with the spirit of fear!

- Continue to ask Jesus for what the good word or message is for this dream until you get it. Do not settle for less than Jesus's best.

Do you know of any parent who would give his hungry child, who asked for food, a plate of rocks instead? ...If you, imperfect as you are, know how to lovingly take care of your children and give them what's best, **how much more ready is your heavenly Father to give wonderful gifts** *to those who ask him?* (Matthew 7:9-11)

Warning dreams are a wonderful opportunity!

Until the event the dream has warned of actually happens, we must make the choice to operate along with fear *or* with God's power. I've learned it is our comfort and joyful response to *establish God's good answer and truth in the situation.*

We have God's Word. Ask, and He will give the right scripture to speak over the dream scenario. This brings His redemption over the dream. God's Word is key. Agree with the knowledge that God is *always* good, no matter what we see happening in the natural.

If there is a death dream, speak life over the person and the family of the person you saw die. My favorite declaration is based on Psalm 118:17: "(This person) will live and not die and declare what the Lord has done!"

The same is true when seeing sickness or any other disaster. Speak God's truth (health, healing, wholeness, peace, and life) over the dream and ask Jesus for His peace to surround you and all who are involved. You are never too young or too old to speak powerful prayers to Jesus. He always hears your prayer and is ready to help.

Notes

Our prayers of agreement with Heaven have power! It is our job to ask for the **good** redemptive word from God in every situation.

Notes

Holy Spirit is standing with you, waiting for your agreement to bring His answer to every difficult issue. The Holy Spirit takes hold of us in our human frailty *to empower us in our weakness*. For example, at times we don't even know how to pray or know the best things to ask for:

> But the Holy Spirit rises up within us to **super-intercede** on our behalf, pleading to God with emotional sighs too deep for words (Romans 8:26).

> *When I need love*
> *I hold out my hands and I touch love.*
> *I never knew there was so much love*
> *Keeping me warm night and day.*
> —"When I Need You," sung
> by Leo Sayer 1977[4]

25

Death of an Issue

25: Being brought to account by the grace of God (5 x 5); expecting grace and mercy (20 + 5); forgiveness (see Matthew 25).

> *I was in what seemed like a funeral home. It was very bright in the room. There were flowers and good things around me. (The setting felt good but seemed the opposite of what I was feeling and seeing.) I was experiencing (effortlessly on my part) what it must be like to be lowered into a casket, then into a grave. Someone was there explaining to me what I was experiencing, although I was not the one who was dead. There were two caskets. I clearly saw two motorized "cranes" that pick up and lower the caskets into the ground. I woke a bit shaken but not fearful of death.*
>
> —STEPH

When a dream involves death, it is easy to automatically believe the worst-case scenario—a friend or family member is going to die. I want to encourage you—*do not jump to this conclusion about a death dream.*

A dream may not be speaking of physical death but rather an issue that needs to "die," a situation that needs to be corrected, or something that needs

Notes

to come to an end so that we can enjoy freedom and live a Spirit-filled life.

Death in a dream may be signaling the end, "death," or correction of:

- a sin or other habit that needs to end;

- a lie that you believed could be exposed and ended;

- a relationship may be changing or ending;

- words used to communicate may need change (see dream below);

- double-mindedness or a heart that is not secure in Jesus;

- end of selfish ways, refusing to demand your own way anymore (see Matt. 10:38);

- death can signify a shift—the end of the old life or old pattern, and the new mindset and joy-filled life is on the way.

For the mind-set of the flesh is death, but the mind-set controlled by the Spirit finds life and peace (Romans 8:6).

My own heart, will, or desires can influence a dream.

Jeremiah states that our *hearts are wicked* and *deceitful above all things* and even that *our heart is extremely sick* (see Jer. 17:9). Jeremiah made quite a statement here and gives us a clue about our selfish tendencies to *get our own way*. Our own *cravings* or *infatuations* may influence our dreams or the interpretation of the dream.

Without realizing it, our own heart may be the problem God wants to help us understand. Because our heart is deceptive and selfish, it is possible to interpret a dream as permission to do wrong, deliberately sin, or enter an unhealthy relationship. We must carefully search out God's thoughts on the dream and listen to wise counsel. Sometimes, God will offend (or irritate) your mind so that you can check your heart.

Important thoughts about these types of dreams:

When considering a death dream, it is important to *speak life* over the person(s) or animals and the situation of death. In other words, declare that the person in the dream will live and not die (see scripture below) and ask for God's blessing and protection over the people you recognize in the dream.

- Write down the dream and follow the normal steps of journaling your dream.

- Refuse to participate with the spirit of fear.

- Look up the person's name who died in your dream in a name dictionary. Their name meaning may be the key to understanding the interpretation.

For example: In a dream a puppy named Odin dies. The name *Odin* means "fury." One possibility could be that God is putting to death the "fury" or anger in your own life. God is setting you free and healing your heart. Or, another possibility is that another person's anger or fury toward you will be ending.

Prayer of Declaration

> *I agree with Jesus, (this person or animal represented in the dream) will live and will not die and will declare the glory (greatness, honor, and majesty) of the Lord! In Jesus's Name.*

Notes

Remember: A dead or dying person may represent a strong issue or mindset that needs to die.

Dream Interpretation

In looking at the dream above, how I felt when waking was important. Instead of being involved with a normal death situation, it was almost like Holy Spirit had taken me into His classroom and I was observing a master teacher at work. I realized that when we give God permission to change our heart He works to accomplish this even in our sleep. God was allowing me to observe how easily He "lays to rest" the works of our own flesh (issues, attitudes, or mindsets)—so much so that it can seem effortless on our part.

The **two caskets** represent Holy Spirit "laying to rest" *two issues* in my life at the same time. He was talking me through the process, revealing how easy it is when we are in agreement with Him. I did not have to work hard for this to happen, but simply partner (or agree) with Him and allow Him to teach me how He was going to accomplish this.

In the dream, the **number two** is repeated, so it is important. There were *two of us*, *two issues* laid to rest, and *two caskets*. *Two* represents the double portion blessing and that I, in *agreement* with Holy Spirit, was *witnessing* and establishing this new place of rest. *Two* may also represent division or double-mindedness. In the dream, God was dealing with my doubt—or lack of trust in what He is doing.

God is able to put to death double-mindedness that allows fear, anger, bitterness, habits, or addictions to rule our lives. We can simply give Him permission then watch and trust as He completes the work.

The Power of Life and Death is in the Tongue

I was watching a boxing match. Jerrod (my husband) was in the ring and his opponent was winning. I watched this fight realizing Jerrod was in trouble as the punches became more vicious. A knockout blow was thrown; Jerrod landed on the canvas so hard I knew he was dead. I woke weeping. —Joanie

Dream Interpretation

The **boxing match** is what is happening in this man's life. A "ring" in which a boxing match is held can be a play on words, revealing that the man is in covenant relationship—in this case, with both his wife and Jesus. Being **punched** or "taking a blow" is like being pummeled with *painful words*. The words can be from a human source or words from the enemy that we begin to believe. Words can kill.

In real life, Joanie, who had the dream, was being called to pray for her husband's life and circumstances to build him up and strengthen him with good words. The redeeming truth is that this husband and wife, together with Jesus, will deliver the knockout punch to the enemy!

> *Your words are so powerful that they will kill or give life* (Proverbs 18:21).

26

Prayer Assignments

26 (20 + 6): Expecting rest; the good news; the gospel, Matthew 26.

> In my dream, I heard a knock at the door. When I answered, a man told me, "George (my husband) is dead." I had no sadness, but felt like it was just a matter of fact.
>
> **Twenty-nine** people from my **family** (church/believers) came over and asked to see George. I told them he had been buried for **three** days (resurrection to life). They brought me a **gift** (salvation) and I placed it on the **mantel** over the **fireplace**, which had a roaring fire in it. (This fire represents God's Presence and my continual prayer for George.) **Yellow flowers** appeared around the **gift** they brought. (The yellow flowers represented the gift clothed with His glory, Matthew 6:28-30.)
>
> —LAURA

Daughter's Dream the Same Night

> I saw my dad (George) in a casket. He was dead, but all of a sudden he opened his eyes, sat up, and began talking to me! I woke shaken.

- **Woke shaken**: the dream triggered the daughter's own need for salvation.

- The daughter "saw" her dad **wake up—** his **spiritual eyes opened** to his need for salvation.

- The mom had been praying for both the father and the daughter to receive Jesus. This gave her the confidence that Holy Spirit was at work and the strength to continue to agree with Heaven in fervent prayer (the **burning fireplace**). She is joined by 29 believers who love her and join her in prayer for her family (20 + 9, waiting, expecting the work of the Holy Spirit).

Remember: A death dream may signal the need for Jesus and His salvation. *Death dreams may be a prayer assignment for a person's salvation.*

When we experience death in a dream, it prompts us to recognize the seriousness of the moment. God is alerting us to speak His life into the situation, agree with His strategy, and have confidence that this person's life and salvation is in Jesus's hands.

In this case, the death dream was an alert to both dreamers. The mother needed to be comforted that God had heard her prayer and confirmed she was to continue to agree with Holy Spirit as He does His work in the husband's heart. Holy Spirit gave this dream to the mother and daughter the same night. This type of double dream was a wake-up call to the daughter and her need to return to Jesus and His love.

> *Haven't you experienced how kind and understanding he [Jesus] has been to you? Don't*

Notes

mistake his tolerance for acceptance. Do you realize that all the wealth of his extravagant kindness is meant to melt your heart and lead you into repentance? (Romans 2:4)

My old identity has been co-crucified with Messiah and no longer lives...the Anointed One lives his life through me—we live in union as one! My new life is empowered by... God who loves me so much that he gave himself for me, and dispenses his life into mine! (Galatians 2:20)

The Source

Truth's shining light guides me in my choices and decisions; the revelation of your word makes my pathway clear. To live my life by your righteous rules has been my holy and lifelong commitment. I'm bruised and broken, overwhelmed by it all; breathe life into me again by your living word. Lord, receive my grateful thanks and teach me more of how to please you. Even though my life hangs in the balance, I'll keep following what you've taught me, no matter what. The ungodly have done their best to throw me off track, but I'll not deviate from what you've told me to do. Everything you speak to me is like joyous treasure, filling my life with gladness. I have determined in my heart to obey whatever you say, fully and forever!

—PSALM 119:105-112

27

The Right Source

27 (20 + 7): **Expecting God's perfection; truth.**

> *In my vision I had access to a large stereo that had a **radio receiver**
> similar to what was popular in the 1980s. On the stereo, there was
> a large **silver tuning knob** that I had my hand on. I was turning the
> silver knob so the radio frequency could be heard, but I was not look-
> ing at the knob; rather, my eyes were **focused on Jesus.** Jesus was
> telling me who I was. As long as I kept my eyes on Him I was able to
> receive and believe what He was saying.*
>
> —MELISSA

The Correct Source for Hearing from the Spirit

The vision above is a wonderful picture of how we hear from the Spirit realm.
A **radio** is a symbolic "picture" of how we can hear news or music in the natural. We have to "tune in" to the Holy Spirit to hear the message, song, art, or
invention Jesus wants to share with us. Melissa had to keep her eyes on Jesus
so she could adjust or tune in to the correct "frequency" or source so she could
clearly "hear" what He was saying.

The **silver knob** (silver represents "redemption," see Exod. 30:11-16) is a metaphor for how we hear from Jesus through His love and sacrifice that brought redemption for us. We "tune in" to the clear, simple, truth frequency.

Radio **static** that would keep you from tuning in to hear the frequency (spirit) correctly is like the enemy's voice that clouds or distorts the truth (see John 10:11-18).

> *My own sheep will hear my voice and I know each one, and they will follow me* (John 10:27).

Note how Melissa was hearing Jesus tell her who she is. This is a sweet picture. Jesus created you like you are and loves you more than anyone. He can only tell the truth about who you are. He is the source to hear from to accurately understand who you are and what your purpose and destiny is.

There Is Power in the Truth

When I was young, I asked for a guitar for my birthday but received a toy guitar instead. I quickly realized there was no benefit to having a plastic version because I did not want to pretend to play; I wanted to really learn to play, which was impossible to do on a cheap imitation.

Jesus wants to give you the genuine Holy Spirit. One line of His truth can change your life for the better forever. The enemy may give information from his realm, but you'll find it is a cheap imitation of the power-filled, accurate revelation from God. Regardless of what others think, you are never too young or too old to learn to hear from the Holy Spirit.

Here are a few of the infinite ways Jesus communicates to us:

- Seeing (with my eyes)

- Hearing

- Smelling

- Tasting

- Sense or touch

- Dreams

- Visions (not quite asleep, but not awake)

- Open visions (similar to seeing a mini movie when awake)

- Daydreams

- Déjà vu

- Prophetic words from a trusted source

- Impressions

- Art and through pictures

- Numbers

- Colors

- Time (like seeing 4:44 on the clock)

- Calendar dates (Hebrew calendar or Gregorian calendar)

- Nature (see Rom. 1:20)

- Animals or pets (see Gen. 30 and 41)

- Natural happenings around me

- My circumstances

Notes

- God's promises, His covenant (see Exod. 24)

- Bible, God's Word

There is no limit on Holy Spirit's forms of communication. God has given us His Word and authenticated it by laying His whole life down for you.

KEY: Stay connected to Jesus and His Word.

He is the correct source for *all* wisdom. If we allow other sources (i.e., our own understanding or a secular worldview that eliminates God) to define our understanding of God, we become confused or doubt His love. Word pictures are a fantastic way to understand God's language, but they never take the place of Scripture.

Keep your eyes focused on Jesus; allow Him to define your dreams and who you are by keeping your "radio" tuned to hear His Spirit frequency. God always confirms His Word.

> *My passion and delight is in your word, for* ***I love what you say to me!*** *I long for more revelation of your truth, for* ***I love the light of your word*** *as I meditate on your decrees* (Psalm 119:47-48).

28

The Wrong Source

28 (20 + 8): Awaiting or expecting a new beginning; Christ in you (see Matthew 28).

One of the blessings of Fire Camp is getting to see into a child's dream life over two or three years. Here is an example of how dreams are affected by positive or negative influences.

The first time we met Sam he was having dreams similar to Daniel of the Bible. His dreams were creative, held excellent revelation, and were full of life-giving, even funny story lines. The next year the dreams became darker and the story lines were disjointed and odd. The following year, Sam's dreams had become tormented and he was having thoughts of suicide. The enemy's influence was obvious as it moved through his life. Sam had gone from being influenced primarily by God's Word and church family to playing games and reading books with content that was not full of life. Sam went from feeling loved to feeling like an outcast within a relatively short period of time.

Be aware of who is influencing you. Popular trends are abundant that lead us to live, believe, and function with evil. I want to encourage you to choose to seek out good influences and to participate with the Holy Spirit, the One who seeks to give life and joy (see 1 Pet. 5:8).

Notes

Who and What You Invite into Your Life Is Powerful

The advance of technology has brought thousands of new options in gaming, both good and not so good. Playing with a Ouija board or going to a psychic opens the door to evil influence into our life.

The decision to use the enemy's resources, even if it seems like a game, sets in motion the law of attraction. Good or evil are set in motion with our agreement. Evil attracts evil, guilt attracts other guilty participants, and the enemy's spirit realm follows with evil thoughts, actions, and behaviors.

How does the enemy work?

One of his favorite tools is fear. He wants to keep you from hearing from Jesus, so he uses anything that causes fear in your life to discourage you and keep you from learning of the things of the Spirit. If you are around those participating with the enemy, reading or watching scary shows, the enemy will magnify whatever scares you. He will be quick remind you of fear you felt when you watched something scary and use it as a trap to keep you from living in freedom.

> When I was in junior high (before I knew Jesus), my friend and I decided to play with a Ouija board. We thought it would be a fun diversion and did not believe it would have any other effect on us; however, the game quickly proved our opinions wrong. We found the game had a dark, evil power that we could not explain. I knew immediately I never wanted to play this "game,"

or whatever it was, again! —Frank, missionary friend

Jesus is always available!

Run to Him; ask Him what to do when confronted with evil! He and all of Heaven are on your side waiting for the invitation to help you overcome the enemy's influence in your life. The angels focus their attention on you and are cheering wildly for your success. They are fiercely fighting the enemy for you, clearing the path for your success. When you run to Jesus, with great compassion He races to meet you, sweeping you up in His arms, hugging you with tender love (see Luke 15:20).

> *Seek good and not evil—and live! You talk about God, the God-of-the-Angel-Armies, being your best friend. ...Hate evil and love good* (Amos 5:14-15 MSG).

Learning to Participate with Good or Evil

When you love someone, you'll do whatever possible to attract them to spend time with you. You will not participate with anything that would disappoint or turn them away. It is the same with Jesus. He lovingly gave us a list of practices to avoid to protect us from evil. Each of these practices carries a strong warning to stay far away from them and those who practice them. Jesus is already madly in love with you, and when you run to Him, He will give you the best answers—just ask!

Here is great news! When we love and join with God He will defeat the enemies who attack us. Our enemies will come at us one way and run away from us seven directions! God will order a blessing on what we do, and He makes us

Notes

prosper. He blesses where we live and what we enjoy (see Deut. 28:7-8 MSG).

God warns against these practices because the end result is meant to destroy us.

Most of these practices are centered on receiving information that captures your curiosity; then this information is used to trap you in doubt, fear, and a destructive thought process.

The purpose of this list is to help you *completely avoid any trap the enemy wants to lay,* keeping you from potential damage and loss in this struggle.

Satan's Tactics

Astrology

Astrology attempts to give credit to the position of the constellations for influencing human characteristics and activities. Signs of the zodiac and horoscopes are charts used to predict the future. God specifically warns against using such devices. *Do not confuse this with astronomy,* which is the good scientific study of heavenly objects (stars, planets, and other heavenly objects).

Clairvoyance

Clairvoyance is using the enemy's supernatural realm to gain information about people, objects, or events. We can always ask Jesus for what we need to know, and He loves to share His thoughts.

Divination

Divination is using objects (tarot cards, tea leaves, sticks, rocks, beans, etc.) in order to find answers instead of asking Jesus.

Enchantment

Enchantment is using a magical spell or charm involving manipulation and selfish goals, not from God.

Exorcism

A religious or spiritual practice for evicting a demon spirit from a person or place. When we love and serve God, we may use Jesus's Name and authority to command a demon spirit to leave (see Mark 16:17-18).

Psychics, Fortunetelling, Soothsaying

These methods of hearing from the spirit world attempt to lay a plan for you that will dictate your life according to the enemy's plan instead of freeing you trust God's good plan for your life and make good decisions with God's leading (see Ps. 23 and 24).

A psychic may give you some truthful information, but this "truth" will be just enough to gain trust, with the goal of laying a trap so you will believe a lie, become fearful, or make a bad decision.

As believers in Jesus we have the ability to hear accurately from the Holy Spirit. He is always available! His answers are good, healthy, and safe.

The correct way to hear from God:

> When someone prophesies [hearing from Holy Spirit], he speaks to encourage people, to build them up, and to bring them comfort (1 Corinthians 14:3).

Witchcraft

Witchcraft and wizardry is manipulation and control using demonic power. Those who practice this enter into the enemy's realm in order to control others for selfish gain. There is no good or "white" witchcraft. It is impossible to

Notes

get good and evil from the same evil source. God strictly forbids this practice (see 1 Sam. 28:3-25; see also *witch doctor*, a counterfeit healer, Exod. 7:11).

Magic

Casting spells, sorcery, or magic is the practice of a person using supernatural power with the aid of evil spirits. The goal of the spell caster is to manipulate a person to do what they want; deception, fear, and curses are the tools of these practices.

Idols

Idols are statues with animal, human, or fantasy likeness. They may look harmless but they may carry a demonic presence. Idols have recently become more popular in home decoration. God strongly warns against idolatry and the first commandment is about refusing to have anything to do with idols. It is a warning to take seriously but carries an amazing blessing when we obey this command (see Exod. 20:3-5).

Our culture has popularized people as "idols" (movie stars, musicians, authority figures, or relationships). A person may become so influential in our life that God must deal with our heart. No human personality should take a more important or influential place than Jesus.

A simple way to check is to ask Holy Spirit, "Who is sitting on the throne in my heart?" He will show you. If it is anyone or anything other than Jesus, ask forgiveness and invite Jesus to take His rightful place in your heart.

Superstition

A superstition gives power to an action (like knocking on wood) or object that on its own does not possess any ability to change reality. For instance, the number 13 may be considered bad luck in the US but in other countries considered a good number that brings good fortune. Remember, whatever we honor (positive or negative) we will give power to. It is important to give honor and power to God instead of to objects or actions.

Activities that involve fear, pain or self-harm

You are precious to Jesus. If you have suffered pain or trauma and the temptation to deal with this comes in the form of inflicting pain on yourself or others, run to Jesus for His help. He knows everything. He is never ashamed or embarrassed of you. He knows everything about you and the thoughts and intentions of your heart even before you do. Tell Him everything and ask for His help. There is also a book available to help with this issue in the resource section at the end of this book.

Drugs

Drugs, alcohol, herbs, or other substances, legal or illegal, alter your reality by your own methods. A "high" experience is a counterfeit and dangerous avenue to experience the supernatural. This can lead you into the enemy's territory and can forever change or damage your life.

God's Truth

The Greek word *dunamis* means dynamic; great power, strength, force, capability; raw power to accomplish something: *"But you shall receive power when the Holy Spirit has come upon you; and you shall be witnesses to Me in Jerusalem, and in all Judea and Samaria, and to the end of the earth"* (Acts 1:8 NKJV). *Dunamis* is a Greek word and where we get the English word *dynamite*.

God wants to release His dunamis power in you so you walk through life working with Him, seeing miracles, signs, and wonders.

Notes

Here is the truth: Our heart and spirit longs to experience the power and Presence of the true supernatural God. We were made this way. If you find yourself wanting to escape reality, simply talk to Jesus. There is no way to get to the true supernatural without Jesus (see John 14:6). We must have our hearts lined up correctly with His or we risk running into dangerous territory.

> *Haven't I already warned you that those who use their "freedom" for these [evil] things will not inherit the kingdom realm of God! But the fruit produced by the Holy Spirit within you is divine love in all its varied expressions: joy that overflows, peace that subdues, patience that endures, kindness in action, a life full of virtue, faith that prevails, gentleness of heart, and strength of spirit. Never set the law above these qualities, for they are meant to be limitless* (Galatians 5:21-23).

If you've already listened to music, read books, played games, or watched movies that have influenced you to agree with evil or trained you in evil activities, I want to encourage you to ask Jesus to forgive you. Jesus is gently but passionately pursuing you and cares deeply about every detail of your life. He is waiting for the invitation to come from you.

The Word of God is like a shield, a very strong protection against the enemy's traps. Stay humble, close to God's Word and His Holy Spirit, and stay close to good influence.

Good is attracted to good—it is that simple. Choose wisely and guard your heart. Refuse to agree with evil thoughts or choices. Remember, God gives you dreams to help you avoid any trap the enemy wants to set for you.

God has given you free will and allows you to make choices, but He will stop at nothing to strongly warn you to stay away from evil.

> *The heart is hopelessly dark and deceitful, a puzzle that no one can figure out. But I, God, search the heart and examine the mind. I get to the heart of the human. I get to the root of things. I treat them as they really are, not as they pretend to be* (Jeremiah 17:9-10 MSG).

Notes

29

Jesus vs. Psychic

29 (20 + 9): Expecting to walk in the gifts of the Spirit; expecting to see God's will be done; holy life expressed in how you live because of what Jesus has done in you.

I overheard two young girls, about 16 years old, having a conversation in a coffee shop. One of the girls had had a dream she was concerned about. Apparently, the girls were consulting an online dream dictionary on their phones. They were questioning how an online dream dictionary could be relevant to their own personal dreams. The online dream interpretation was vague and did not seem relevant to the highly personal dream. They realized the train of thought was based in man's thought or intellect and did not answer the personal heart issues of the dream. (Very wise!) Questioning how impersonal the online information was, together the girls concluded, "Maybe I should make an appointment to see a psychic."

The goal of this chapter is to tell you the truth about the two spirit realms.

One of the most important tools I can give you concerning dream interpretation is understanding of the spirit realm so that you will never be tempted to turn to a psychic for any type of spiritual understanding or dream interpretation. The undercurrent of this chapter is full of love and the strength of God's Word.

We were created to hear from God's Spirit realm.

God made us with a built-in Spirit receiver and His plan was for us to hear His heart, His thoughts, and His will from His Holy Spirit (see 1 Cor. 14:3).

True dream interpretation is Holy Spirit revealing God's heart and unique plan for you.

The enemy gained access to our realm when Adam and Eve sinned. Man listened to the enemy instead of believing God's Word. If people who literally walked with God on the earth daily could be deceived, we must carefully guard who we give access to our hearts and minds.

Receiving Truth from Our Built-in Gift of Revelation

The receiver and transmitter of information we have common access to is a cell tower that houses communication equipment. These receivers allow us to enjoy wireless communication on our cell phones, computers, and wireless Internet.

When we "receive" information from the spirit realm, it is vitally important that we carefully discern who the source is behind the information. We can receive good, life-giving information from a safe, godly source, or we can go to someone who claims to receive signals from the spirit but refuses godly boundaries of the Holy Spirit.

Notes

A psychic is one who downloads information from the enemy.

Receiving tainted information from a psychic is similar to downloading a destructive virus on your computer. It has come from a dangerous source meant to trap you with information that holds half-truths and leads to uncertainty and chaos.

Can a psychic hear truth?

Dark forces are looking for a place to send a signal. A psychic has the ability to receive a signal and hear information and give direction. This gift originally came from God (because He is the only Creator), but instead of choosing to hear God's signal, they turned away from God and have chosen to receive or tune in to an enemy channel that has an evil and dark source.

The Difference Between a Prophet and a Psychic

Jesus said:

> *I am the **Good Shepherd**. I know my own sheep [you and I] and my own sheep know me. In the same way, the Father knows me and I know the Father. I put the sheep before myself, sacrificing myself if necessary. ...They'll also recognize my voice* (John 10:14-16 MSG).

A *psychic* has chosen to hear from a different, evil signal. Psychics, mediums, clairvoyants, witches, sorcerers, and those participating in various "magic arts" are searching for the enemy's information and plan, regardless of how selfish, dark, or destructive it is. It is possible that this person began with a gift or ability to hear from God's spirit realm, but instead of learning from the Holy Spirit he turned his "receiver" to hear the enemy's voice.

The enemy is always looking for a way to steal and pervert God's spiritual gifts. A psychic may believe he is the one in control of calling on dark forces, but he is a slave to manipulation of the enemy who he is trying to get information from.

Dark spirits want to destroy you and will use any trick or lie that they can to trap you with. No matter how popular our culture makes the dark spirit realm, the goal is always the same. The enemy's plan is to destroy your life. If you follow a psychic's advice, you will be following and agreeing with the enemy's plan to destroy your life.

When you consult with a psychic or a witch, you are asking a demon for answers instead of God's wisdom. The enemy will take any door left open as an invitation to bring in every kind of darkness. This is what Jesus said:

> *A hired man [psychic and those operating with dark forces] is not a real **shepherd**. The sheep [you and I] mean nothing to him. He sees a wolf [demonic force, enemy] come [to destroy us, the sheep] and runs for it, leaving the sheep to be ravaged and scattered by the wolf. He's only in it for the money. The sheep don't matter to him* (John 10:12-13 MSG).

> *Sin is a dethroned monarch [king]; so you must no longer give it an opportunity to rule over your life, **controlling how you live** and **compelling you to obey its desires and cravings**. So then, **refuse to answer its call** to surrender your body as a tool for wickedness. Instead, **passionately answer God's call** to keep yielding your body to Him as one who*

Notes

159

*has now experienced resurrection life! You live now for his pleasure, ready to be used for his noble purpose. **Remember this: sin will not conquer you*** (Romans 6:12-14).

When we obey God, He will put His angels and blessing over us! He will war against the enemy and bring peace to our home and to our sleep.

I choose to hear from the Good Shepherd and not hear the voice of another (see John 10:14). I will guard this gift of hearing from God's Holy Spirit realm (see 2 Tim. 1:14). Dreams are a treasure. Hearing from the Holy Spirit is a gift.

The enemy is warring through every means possible, especially popular culture, to steal or tempt you to compromise the gift God has given you. Just as you would carefully guard a priceless diamond, protect and treasure this generous gift. Ask Holy Spirit to help you use this gift as He intended, with a humble heart and much joy so that Jesus will always be glorified!

Remember: Dreams are an on-ramp to a highway—a higher way to understanding God's thoughts and ways—or an airport runway that gives you the ability to go to a higher, heavenly realm to hear God's thoughts. I am a receiver of God's revelation and choose to listen to His Holy Spirit.

You make me bold! I can hear Your voice and live confidently in Your Word. Jesus, You always have my very best in mind!

Remember: The gifts of God are irrevocable. In other words, even if you choose to use the gifts He has given you in a wrong way, God will not take back what He has given you. God created us with the ability to tune in to the spirit realm. God's gift of free will affords all of us the ability to hear from the Spirit; it is our choice to use it for good or evil (see Rom. 11:29; Matt. 5:45).

Notes

This Is War

When you sit enthroned under the shadow of Shaddai [God, the Destroyer of Enemies], you are hidden in the strength of God Most High. He's the hope that holds me and the Stronghold to shelter me, the only God for me, and my great confidence. He will rescue you from every hidden trap of the enemy, and he will protect you from false accusation and any deadly curse. His massive arms are wrapped around you, protecting you. You can run under his covering of majesty and hide. His arms of faithfulness are a shield keeping you from harm. You will never worry about an attack of demonic forces at night nor have to fear a spirit of darkness coming against you. Don't fear a thing! Whether by night or by day, demonic danger will not trouble you, nor will the powers of evil launched against you. Even in a time of disaster, with thousands and thousands being killed, you will remain unscathed and unharmed. you will be a spectator as the wicked perish in judgment, for they will be paid back for what they have done! When we live our lives within the shadow of God Most High, our secret hiding place, we will always be shielded from harm. How then could evil prevail against us or disease infect us? God sends angels with special orders to protect you wherever you go, defending you from all harm. If you walk into a trap, they'll be there for you and keep you from stumbling. You'll even walk unharmed among the fiercest powers of darkness, trampling every one of them beneath your feet! For here is what the Lord has spoken to me: "Because you have delighted in me as my great lover, I will greatly protect you. I will set you in a high place, safe and secure before my face. I will answer your cry for help every time you pray, and you will find and feel my Presence even in your time of pressure and trouble. I will be your glorious hero and give you a feast. You will be satisfied with a full life and with all that I do for you. For you will enjoy the fullness of my salvation!"

—Psalm 91 MSG

30

Two Kingdoms

30: Right timing (3 x 10); carries the meaning of perfection or divine order; family.

> I was sleeping soundly. As I slept, I felt the gentle breeze of what felt like angel wings just above me. Although I could not see the wings (as I slept), I could sense they were about 10-12 inches thick, longer than six feet, a rainbow spectrum of color and light, very large but weightless. When I woke it seemed the air around me was charged with health, strength, and joy.
> —STEPH

This angelic encounter infused confidence into my life that is unshakeable. Whether I feel it or not, I know that every day, God's angelic realm is continually around me. I do not have these experiences as frequently as I would like, but I am constantly paying attention to what Jesus is doing around me.

These enjoyable experiences are part of the normal believer's Kingdom life. We carry the tangible Presence of God. When we are young, it is easy to engage with this heavenly realm because it has not been discouraged by doubt and disbelief.

Jesus spoke of His Kingdom more than any other subject while on earth. I pray that God's Kingdom understanding will be open to you now and never be shut off by unbelief.

Two Kingdoms: The Original Game of Thrones

There are two kings at war for your life. Both kings have a plan for you. The choice you make is unlike any other decision. The direction you choose will affect your life for all of eternity.

God's Kingdom Characteristics

- God's government is based on liberty.

- God's gift is His Word so we know how to walk in freedom, full of His Spirit, bringing His Kingdom benefits and creativity to earth.

- God created us like Himself.

- We were given the amazing gift of free will. There cannot be true obedience without the ability to disobey.

- God's Kingdom is literally righteousness, peace, and joy in the Holy Spirit (Rom. 14:17).

- We are successful in Jesus, simply because we love Him and He loves us. There is nothing we can do to make Him love us more or less.

I am God's child. I live in His Kingdom. I carry His Presence.

- This King loves you and is fully motivated to see you experience His love. He left all He had in Heaven, lived and experienced life on earth, and laid down His own life so you could live with Him.

- We can come boldly before our Father God's throne in Heaven, asking for His help.

- Jesus is the best friend you'll ever have and closer than your closest sibling.

- Jesus has perfect love for you that eradicates all fear and gives you boldness and confidence to live out your destiny.

- Holy Spirit will lead us into all truth, knowledge, and wisdom. He is the best teacher you'll ever know. When we ask, He will open up any subject we are interested in with genius beyond earthly understanding.

- We are given the mind of Christ and therefore must participate with Holy Spirit to understand His thoughts to the world. Agreeing with Heaven for God's plan will shift individuals, leaders, systems, and nations into God's truth (see 1 Cor. 2). You have the ability to pray and see a nation change.

- We are blessed with angelic help and comfort (see Ps. 91:11).

- We are protected and hidden in His Presence (see Ps. 91).

Notes

- We walk in His forgiveness, which brings freedom from all sin and the shame it brings.

- Our job is to prepare for God's Kingdom that is to come. There is so much more ahead; we can only begin to imagine the joy. The future just gets better and brighter for this Kingdom!

- This Kingdom has the promise that you will live eternally and Jesus will reign as King!

*You will show me the path of life; **in Your Presence is fullness of joy;** at Your right hand are pleasures forevermore* (Psalm 16:11 NKJV).

Note: I do not like to think or speak of the enemy. We live in a time when popular culture makes the enemy's kingdom deceptively compelling. With this in mind, it is necessary to give clarity to the enemy's plan for you and expose the truth about his kingdom.

Satan's Kingdom

His goal is to bring you under his power and control, and he will use whatever method necessary to trap you into thinking like him. He does not care about the outcome of your life and does not consider your safety.

- This kingdom leads to death and its foundation is based in *lies* and *cheap imitation.*

- This kingdom is inferior, destructive, and full of the opposite characteristics of God's Kingdom.

The **foundation** of God's Kingdom is His Presence!

- This king has only selfish motives and wants you to follow his lead down a path toward increased control and eventual captivity.

- He is the ultimate counterfeiter—he is a created being that has no ability to create, only imitate.

- Although he has no ability to create, he is quick to take credit for what God has created, setting in motion numerous lies like the theory of evolution, which has brought a confusing narrative to science and has muddled true history.

- He deceives entire nations and people groups with false religions and beliefs.

- Entire systems (government, science, economics, media, business, and education) are perverted from their original intent of bringing safety, truth, and righteous leadership and prosperity to the world and instead participate in corruption of truth.

- The owner of this evil kingdom will keep us busy chasing after worthless things that never satisfy, distracting us from accomplishing our true destiny.

- His kingdom is full of jealousy, manipulation, and addictions to a multitude of substances (food, drugs, and evil actions like stealing).

The difference between these two kingdoms is profound.

You are important in God's Kingdom and you are His favorite one! The biggest hope I carry is that I will meet you there one day where we will laugh, sing, whistle, holler, jump, stomp, run to see Jesus together!!

- The enemy may promise you fame and fortune, but these are a temporary counterfeit.

- His goal is to destroy. He wants us to be out of control and rebellious to any type of law so he can set chaos in motion, followed by death and destruction wherever possible.

- Finally, this kingdom is spiraling toward eternal death.

The very best news I have about this kingdom is that soon it will end and its master will be sent to eternal torment, never to resurface!

Jesus left us with the Holy Spirit to build God's Kingdom.

When Jesus left this earth, He commanded the disciples to take the gospel to the whole earth, but first *wait* in Jerusalem *until the Holy Spirit was poured out* on them in Acts 2. Not only did He leave the Kingdom building to us, He commanded that we use *His gifts and tools* to accomplish this.

- Tool list: gifts that build, strengthen, and improve with use (see Rom. 12:6-8; 1 Cor. 12:8-10).

- Fruit List: attributes that increase with Holy Spirit (Gal. 5:22-23).

Dreams, visions, and prophecy are three of the specific tools God has chosen to use to draw people into His Kingdom in this hour.

I have found in David...a man who always pursues my heart and will accomplish all that I have destined him to do (Acts 13:22).

Notes

Choose this day whom you will serve.

31

The Invitation

31 (30 + 1): Part of a family; divine order.

> I am looking at a dead tree in my front yard and thinking about cutting it down. I notice the roots of the tree are exposed. Although the tree is dead, the roots have grown into the shape of a pig. My neighbor, whom I do not like, comes over and offers to purchase the pig-shaped roots for $1,000.00.
> —JAMES

James's Dream Interpreted

The above dream is from a man who, presently, does not like God and does not want to accept Jesus into his life.

In the dream, the "neighbor" is Jesus. The "tree" is James's life without Jesus. God is exposing his "roots" as dead and *shaped like a pig*, which symbolizes the man's own life and the junk (sin) that he is holding on to. Even when offered $1,000.00, James does not want to give up his sin (represented by the pig) because he does not like his neighbor, Jesus. One thousand is a significant number. When we choose to love Jesus, His mercy covers us and our family to 1,000 generations (see Deut. 7:9).

This dream is a parable invitation to this man to experience salvation. Jesus is offering to take his sin, forgive him, and bless his family for a very long time. The man has free will and must make the choice for himself.

A dream has the potential of bringing you to Jesus or exposing a hardened heart against Him. We have the amazing gift of free will.

> If we confess our sins, He is faithful and just to forgive us our sins and to cleanse us from all unrighteousness. If we say that we have not sinned, we make Him a liar, and His word is not in us (1 John 1:9-10 NKJV).

Dreams expose our heart and can reveal whether we love or hate God. Dreams expose our fears, our doubts, and our weaknesses as well as give us courage, hope, and direction.

Here is a dream from a young man with an entirely different outcome.

> I was on a long **journey,** a trip around the world that would last **80 hours**. I was searching for a **great treasure**. I knew where I was going, but everywhere I went I was searching for this treasure. I searched all night long then woke up.
> —JACK, age 10

Notes

Jack's Dream Interpreted

Life is an exciting *journey*. A typical lifespan is about *80 years* (represented by 80 hours). The *great treasure* we are searching for is Jesus and His destiny and purpose for our lives (see Luke 12:34; Col. 2:2-4).

In Jack's dream, God was reminding him of the decision he needed to make to draw close to Jesus. Although Jack was a pastor's son and had been around Christians all of his life, he had not personally made the decision to follow Jesus. Because of the dream, he was ready to choose and immediately made the choice to follow Jesus. Another thought—the number of hours Jack traveled was 80 (8 x 10). The number 8 can represent a new beginning, and 10 is the number of complete. This was Jack's opportunity to make a *multiplied, complete new beginning*. Jesus always gives more than we can imagine!

Do I need to choose to follow Jesus?

You were created to live forever and given the amazing gift of free will. You may choose to live close to God or far from Him. One day your physical body will die, but your spirit will continue to live either with God or exist in eternity without Him.

Don't all roads lead to God?

My husband's family owns a wonderful piece of land in a very remote area. In order to get to this land, you have to drive down a certain highway a set number of miles, then make the correct turns down a series of crossroads. The further you continue driving, the more remote and narrow the roads become. There are several forks in the road where you must make the correct road choices or you will not make it to your destination.

Do all roads lead to this destination in the country? No. I must take the correct road and follow directions. If I do not, I will not make it to where I want to be.

Jesus came to earth as a baby and lived on the earth just as you are alive right now. He gave us the correct way to get to His Kingdom and to His own home (see Matt. 7:14). Love shows you the correct way. It would be very unkind to tell someone they can get to their destination by taking any road they choose.

Jesus made the statement that He alone is the way to eternal life. You have easy access to Him, but He gave you freedom to make our own choice.

> *Jesus said, "I am the Road, also the Truth, also the Life. No one gets to the Father apart from me"* (John 14:6 MSG).

Notes

32

Offending Our Mind to Check Our Heart

32 (30 + 2): God's perfect timing + agreement or multiplication.

Presidents' Day, February 20, 2017

*I was with two friends outside on a green field. We were spread out like each of us needed "elbow room." It seemed there was some type of exercise we had to do (not difficult, but good and practical). It was noticeably green outside. Rose had loaned me her set of "open heaven" CDs. I did not know of the CDs (or remember having them) but was willing to look for them. I knew there were 12 CDs in the set (God's governmental number). Rose wanted me to return the CDs because she feared I'd lost them. She did not seem very happy with me, but did not get angry. I was puzzled, not knowing what or where the CDs were. A storm came and we scattered quickly. I went home to search for the CDs. I woke **feeling** as if I had been accused and knew someone was **offended** at me.*

—STEPH

God allows our mind to feel offense to reveal what is in our heart.

In a dream, God has our attention so that He can give us information we need to hear, whether we want to hear it or not. Learn to realize your emotions are powerful purveyors of God's message to you.

Dreams do not come from our own thought processes.

Psychology has tried to explain away dreams as our own rational mind trying to work through issues in our lives. One famous psychologist concluded dreams can only be interpreted through one very narrow subject—physical appetite.

Dreams are creative far beyond our own human understanding and draw us out of our own human intelligence. God speaks to us through a dream parable that we could not come up with on our own, and speaks His thoughts that we may not otherwise be able to hear.

In a dream, God bypasses:

- Our intellect

- Our arguments

- Our religious beliefs

- Our secular or worldly beliefs

- Our own wants or demands

- Our attitude and opinions

- Untruths we've believed or have been taught

Remember: When we are asleep, our body rests deeply. Our breathing slows, our heart rate slows, our mind is not distracted by events or circumstances. Our natural inclination to explain away a dream message is disarmed so that the dream can effectively bring positive change in our life.

I am smart. Why do I need God to tell me what a dream means?

Secular dream understanding contends that dreams come from within our own psyche to bring correction. If this were true, our culture would have fewer serious issues. Instead, evil is on the increase, people do what is right in their own eyes, being self-righteous and not concerned with the harm they cause others.

God sees us from a different standpoint than we see ourselves. He has superior understanding of absolutely every detail of our own mind and will. This is why we turn to God for His understanding and revelation of the dream.

> The heart is **deceitful** above all things and it is extremely sick; who can understand it fully and know its secret motives? (Jeremiah 17:9 AMP)

Dream Interpretation

The dream above was my dream, so it was about me and my heart. It is important to note this so we are careful to not blame others when a dream is dealing with our own feelings.

One of the character traits I'm working on in my life is to *never* be offended at anyone and, of course, I do not want to *cause* offense. After I had the dream, I began to prepare my heart by talking to Jesus about the dream and asking for His wisdom. Soon there was a situation similar to the elements of the dream that I was able to better understand. Because of the dream I was able to maneuver the problem *without* participating with offense. This was possible because the dream alerted me to what was happening in advance so I could prepare my heart and be careful with words that I might speak. Here is more insight into the meaning of the dream:

Presidents' day: This day honors our governmental leadership. God, the perfect governmental leader, is alerting me that He is involved in this situation (see Rom. 13:1).

The number 12: A governmental number. This number was repeated *so I will pay close attention* to the dream.

Two friends: One offended friend, the other a witness to what happened. Jesus is the closest friend we will ever have. He is a witness to all of our actions (see Matt. 18:16).

Rose: This friend's name has significance. Rose can represent the Church. Rose is part of the body of Christ (church) and how I treat her is important because Jesus died for all of us, His church.

Elbow room: The actual problem the dream was alerting me to was that this friend was needing space (elbow room) to mature in ministry. My job was to freely allow her room (and encourage her) and not be offended (green) by this.

The color green: Have you heard the term "green with envy"? When something is repeated, pay close attention. My journal noted that there was *green everywhere*. There were *multiple opportunities* to be offended in this situation. It helped me be very careful to guard my heart against becoming offended or offending my friend. Green also represents *growth*. I have the opportunity to grow and mature because of this situation.

CDs: This element was repeated multiple times, which is a clue to pay attention. A compact disc is a recorded program or a possibly represents a *way of thinking* (see Rom. 12:2). God was dealing with my mind and my heart so that

Notes

I would not react to this situation with my mind, will, or emotions but rather allow Him to help me operate in the opposite spirit of love, joy, peace, and gentleness (see Gal. 5:22).

A CD can also represent a "teaching being loaded" into your heart (see 2 Tim. 2:2). This was Jesus, teaching me how to love others as well as how to not operate in offense.

Storm: The situation happened quickly, similar to a storm. Had I not been alerted by the dream, the situation may have been a difficult "storm" in my life. I was able to talk to Jesus about my own heart in advance, which also alerted me to be very careful of words, thoughts, actions, and prevented much difficulty.

Because of this dream, clarity was brought to the issue in advance. God highlighted and repeated all of the important components of the story so I would catch the lesson. I was able to ask Jesus how to pray for Rose and encourage her without participating in an offense that could have destroyed relationship.

> *Trust in the Lord completely, and do not rely on your own opinions. With all your heart rely on him to guide you, and he will lead you in every decision you make* (Proverbs 3:5).

33

This Is War

33: Religion sets us back, but relationship with the Father, Son, and Holy Spirit is the complete and perfect rule of God.

> *I have this dream every night. There is a man coming at me. He is attacking me and wants to kill me. I have a sword in my hand, and when he attacks me I stab him. He keeps coming after me. There is blood everywhere. I am terrified!*
> —DINESH, age 13

Jesus Makes Us Brave

While in India, Dinesh and four or five of his friends came to me after our Fire Camp dream class. Although we had been working through our dreams in the meeting, Dinesh had been afraid to share his dream publicly. He said, "I have stopped going to sleep at night because I fear I am going to kill a man." He proceeded to tell me his reoccurring dream (above). As Dinesh spoke, he was physically shaking as he recalled the intense feelings that accompanied the dream. Each time he had the dream, he would wake covered in sweat, panicked, and crying out for help.

Immediately, Holy Spirit dropped the interpretation into my heart. "Dinesh, you are not going to kill anyone! The Holy Spirit is trying to help you kill the things in your soul that are trying to kill you! You are learning to use *God's Word* (sword) to defeat (kill) the enemy, and Jesus will help you! Jesus *blood* is covering you because you are His. You can use His Name, His lifeblood, and His Word and authority to stop the enemy. You can do this with boldness and disable every tool of fear the enemy has."

> For we have the living Word of God, which is full of energy, and it **pierces more sharply than a two-edged sword.** It will even **penetrate to the very core** of our being where soul and spirit, bone and marrow meet! It **interprets** and **reveals** the true **thoughts** and **secret motives** of our hearts (Hebrews 4:12).

You can be bold because you are a child of the Most High God, King of the ultimate Kingdom! You have bold access to the Throne of God and His justice. You are a chosen one and as part of the chosen generation you live under a blessing covering. God has given you the mind of Christ—He is for you, never against you! You are highly favored, holy, and He and His life is increasing in you daily. You are seated with Him and share His authority.

These young men had uncommon boldness and wisdom.

> God gave these four young men **knowledge** and **skill** in both books and life. In addition, Daniel was gifted in understanding all sorts of visions and dreams. At the end

*of the time set by the king for their train-ing, the head of the royal staff brought them in to Nebuchadnezzar. When the king inter-viewed them, he found them **far superior to all the other young men**. None were a match for Daniel, Hananiah, Mishael, and Azariah* (Daniel 1:17-19 MSG).

The Hebrew word for "knowledge" here is *madda*, which carries the meaning of God's intelligence or knowl-edge and the understanding of His Presence.

These young men were seriously obedient to God no matter what the circumstances (remember the lion's den and fiery furnace). In this obedience and faithfulness God accelerated their ability to understand His thoughts and increased their depth of wisdom, and Nebuchadnezzar ele-vated them in government.

When you love God, you have access to the same wisdom, intelligence, and brilliance that Daniel and his friends had.

Nebuchadnezzar answered Daniel, and said:

"Your God is beyond question the God of all gods, the Master of all kings. And he solves all mysteries, I know, because you've solved this mystery." Then the king promoted Daniel to a high position in the kingdom, lavished him with gifts, and made him governor over the entire province of Babylon and the chief in charge of all the Babylonian wise men. At Daniel's request the king appointed Shadrach, Meshach, and Abednego to administrative posts throughout Babylon, while Daniel gov-erned from the royal headquarters (Daniel 2:46-49 MSG).

Notes

The way you counsel and correct me makes me praise you more, for your whispers in the night give me wisdom, showing me what to do next (Psalm 16:7).

Defeating the Terrorist

34: God's complete rule and direction in your life (30); north, east, south, and west (4).

> While at the theater, **terrorists** came in with their guns, aimed and shooting. I took cover in a room with **three armed men**. **Three children** had given me their **toy guns** for safekeeping. There I was, in a **room** (Joy's heart) with three men and their **three working guns** and I was holding three toy rifles. I was not the least bit concerned about my safety nor was I afraid to die.
> —JOY

A terrorist represents the enemy, satan, the devil, and demons.

The dream above could have caused Joy to participate with fear, but instead she knew who she was being protected by—*three armed men* (representing Father, Son, and Holy Spirit or angels that represent them) and was confident she was safe. The three working guns they were using represent the effective Word of God that protects us from the enemy's attack. *Three children* represent the promises God has given Joy, and even though the guns given her seem like *toys* (immature weapons) she is positioned well, knowing who she is in Christ, hidden, safe, and with no fear of what may happen next.

Notes

Negative Experiences

Are you struggling with any of these events?

- unable to sleep well or sleep soundly all night long

- night terrors or any other sleep disorder

- not wanting to go to sleep because you fear bad dreams

- being woken up in the middle of the night by unexplained happenings, noises, or voices

- being attacked by something you cannot see or explain

- having panic or anxiety attacks

When we choose Jesus as the One we serve, He gives us the power to use His Word to stop the enemy's plans and trouble.

When I have a dream that wakes me and I'm feeling fearful, I immediately pray:

*Jesus, I am feeling fear because of the dream. I **will not** participate with the spirit of fear. I ask You, Jesus, to remove the fear from me so that it does not affect me or my decisions. You have given me a Spirit of love, power, and sound mind. I choose to participate with **Your thoughts** and **Your power and love, Jesus.***

Steps to eradicate night terror and negative supernatural experiences:

Always speak to Jesus first. Here are some basic steps to eradicate the enemy's attack, but Jesus is fully aware of your particular situation. He has the best and final answer.

1. Ask Jesus for forgiveness for trusting or agreeing with anything that is in opposition to Him.

2. Ask Holy Spirit to help to reveal what is happening.

3. Check your life. Are you participating with anything that gives permission for the enemy to access your life?

4. Walk through your room, asking Holy Spirit to help you find anything (books, games, pictures, toys, hobbies, crafts) that is offensive to Him.

   - When something catches your attention as a possible problem, remove it from your room and your home (if possible) and ask Jesus to spiritually clean up the problem.

   - Search your room and your heart often; this is a lifelong habit.

5. Trust Holy Spirit and the "check" He puts in your heart. Refuse to read, play, or listen to anything that is offensive to Him.

   - This may take some help from your parents.

Notes

Notes

- Honor your parents. Speak to them before getting rid of property unless you purchased it with money you earned.

6. *Ask Jesus* to help you be strong and courageous. If you are tempted to return to the issue that caused the problem, run to Jesus instead. He will help you.

7. Here is the most powerful tool! *God's Word!*

- Repeat or memorize Psalm 91, which has been included in the front of this section.

- Write out this scripture and put it somewhere where you can see and read it; repeat it out loud when possible.

Here is the truth. The Lord will wrap you in His strong love and shield you from all evil. Pray for yourself by placing your hand on your head.

> *I agree with God's Word that every sleep problem I've experienced is now ending. I call upon the powerful and effective lifeblood of Jesus to heal me from all trauma and fear. There will be no opportunity for any type of fear or trauma to enter my life again. From this time on, I agree that I am covered with God's strength, boldness, and courage. Every fear that has been activated against me must stop, now, in Jesus's Name. I ask for the Presence of the Lord to flood my room and surround me like a wall of fire. The effects of trauma or sickness cannot come near me because of the Lord's Presence. I thank You, Lord, for the angel army that You have sent to stand guard around me. Thank You, Jesus, for being my strong*

help in time of need. I love You and thank You for guarding my life. I know You give me, Your beloved one, sleep. In Jesus's Name, amen.

Remember: Even when a dream looks negative, always look for the good or redemptive word in your dream.

Notes

Famous and Creative Dreams

God is a Creator, an innovator and an Inventor and we were created in His image and in His likeness. John 1:3 proclaims, "All things were created through Him, and without Him nothing was created that was created." I believe this is still true; and that witty inventions, technologies, scientific breakthroughs and other innovations that make a positive impact on society are inspired by His Spirit, even if the inventor does not yet know Him.

—JENNIFER LeCLAIRE[5]

35

Daydreams and Déjà Vu

35 (30 + 5): Perfect + grace.

The well-known author of *A Christmas Carol* and *Oliver Twist*, Charles Dickens, told of an interesting occurrence of déjà vu. He became tired one day and decided to take a nap. Just as soon as he fell asleep, he began to dream about a young girl wearing a red shawl.

This young woman spoke four words in the dream, "I am Miss Napier." Later that evening, Dickens was at a social event and a young girl wearing a red shawl was introduced to him as…Miss Napier.

What Is Déjà Vu?

Déjà vu is the feeling or sense that you have already experienced a place, an event, or a conversation that is actually happening for the first time. It is a French word that literally means "already seen."

Months before traveling to India, I began dreaming, almost nightly, that I was somewhere not familiar to me, working with people I had never met. I would wake, puzzled, wondering where was I and what I was doing in these dreams but had no specific dream story to write down.

After arriving in India, on four specific occasions, I had four simple but specific déjà vu experiences:

1. A conversation standing in a circle with new friends I'd never met before.

2. Looking at a very large river.

3. Crossing a certain type of bridge.

4. Being in a specific home.

During each déjà vu experience, I'd pause and think *I've already been here* or *this is familiar* when, in reality, I had never met the people or visited the places. The experiences were not notable in any way, but in my own heart the experience built confidence to know that God had gone before and prepared the path for me. Most importantly, I knew I was in the right place at the right time, meeting the right people.

In my dreams, God had been preparing me to accomplish His purpose and to have confidence He was guiding me. In this case, the déjà vu experiences were comforting and brought peace to the journey.

What should you do when you experience déjà vu?

- Make a note of the experience in your dream journal.

- Take a moment to thank Jesus for His protection and guidance.

Remember: God may allow us to see a glimpse of an event or meet a person in a dream to bring confidence that He knows and directs our life.

Clarification about déjà vu.

In our culture today, some claim that déjà vu is an experience from a past life. This is *not* biblical. You were born in this time and place and have no past earthly life.

Some religions claim you you'll get more chances to make right choices after this life. Do not be confused by this idea.

Here is the truth: When you die, you will go to Heaven and be with Jesus forever. If you reject Him as your Lord, your soul will experience eternal separation from Jesus.

Remember: The choice to love and serve Jesus and be a part of His Kingdom is the most important choice you can make on this earth.

Daydreams

Daydreams occur when your thoughts are allowed to drift, giving your imagination time to work on its own for a few uninterrupted minutes. These moments of quiet reflection are healthy and give you opportunities to explore ideas, remember and enjoy fun past experiences, or consider future potential. It is very possible that God will initiate a daydream.

Can daydreams be useful?

In a nine-week after-school study performed by psychologists, students were given time to imagine academic futures they wanted to achieve and then practice the skills they would need to achieve this. By the end of the school year, the daydreaming students reported:

1. a greater concern about doing well in school,

2. strategies for actually realizing their dreams,

3. stronger emotional well-being, and

4. better attendance.

The students began to look at their goals in a more positive and balanced way. Fear of failure became less important and even behavioral problems were significantly reduced.

Make a habit of unplugging.

When possible, take a break from the barrage of incoming information, find a quiet place, and simply engage in thought. It is surprising how a wellspring of creativity can grow.

Einstein, Newton, and C.S. Lewis were major daydreamers as young people. Some of the most creative ideas of all time have come from night dreams or daydreams.

In her book *Developing Your Five Spiritual Senses*, Patricia King reveals that she was called to preach during a daydream. When the daydream actually came true, the Lord said to her, "This is that daydream coming to pass."[6]

Daydreaming is another God-given ability that makes you unique and gives your life purpose and meaning.

Bring back a night dream by daydreaming.

During the day an event may trigger a memory of a night dream. Ask Jesus for His help, then focus on what you do remember of the dream and spend some time daydreaming. This may help recall the dream that could have otherwise been lost.

36

Do Animals Dream?

36: **Learning to work with God's Kingdom as opposed to building your own (1 Kings 10:19-20); God's perfect government or rule (12 x 3 = 36).**

We were practicing the Presence of Jesus in one of the classes in Fire Camp. The assignment was to lie down and listen to soaking worship music and ask Jesus to show you what is on His heart right now. Within two minutes, Spencer popped up and said:

> *"I saw my puppy! He was running and playing with my grandpa! The grass! The grass was light! Everything was so alive! The light was coming up from under the grass! The flowers were full of light and music! My puppy was so happy!"*
> —SPENCER, age 5

This encounter brought healing and peace to Spencer, who, unbeknownst to us, had recently lost his puppy to some unknown illness. His joy was immediately restored just knowing the puppy he loved was waiting for him safely in Heaven and his beloved family in Heaven was enjoying the puppy. In less than two minutes, Spencer experienced Jesus's heart lovingly focused on Spencer and his puppy and the joy of Heaven.

Jesus loves your animals more than you possibly can because He created them. It brings Him pleasure to see you enjoy and befriend His creation. God made animals with characteristics similar to us so we can learn how to better treat others and have a tangible example of unconditional love.

Do Animals Dream?

If you have a pet, you've probably observed some funny sleeping moments with them. Dogs seem to bark, run, and jump in their sleep. Cats purr, walk and jump. Birds have been known to sing, and practice their daily tasks all while sound asleep.

Aristotle wrote in *The History of Animals*, "It would appear that not only do men dream, but horses also, and dogs, and oxen…sheep, and goats, and all viviparous quadrupeds (four-footed mammals); and dogs show their dreaming by barking in their sleep."[7]

MIT researchers have found that animals have complex dreams and their dreams are connected to actual experiences. Sleeping animals have brain activity similar to humans and go through stages of REM sleep. Animals continue "practice" tasks and routines during sleep that they learn while awake.

While recording the brain activity of zebra finches, researchers found that the sleeping birds practiced their song. The neurons in their brains fired in order, as if the bird was audibly singing the song, note for note.

What the Bible Says about Animals

- God lovingly created every animal for His enjoyment. He called them good and commanded them to multiply and fill the earth (see Gen. 1:21-28; Rev. 4:11).

- God holds the lives of animals in His hands and protected them through the worldwide destruction of the flood (see Job 12:10; Gen. 8:17).

- God cares for them and does not forget about them (see Matt. 10:29; Luke 12:6).

- Those who treat animals kindly are called "righteous" and those who mistreat animals are judged as "cruel" (see Prov. 12:10).

- Jesus seems to really love horses as they are mentioned more than 150 times in the Bible. One day, Jesus will return on a horse (see Rev. 19–21 and Isa. 11:6-9).

37

Famous Dreams

37: Six days of work bring us to seven (rest); learning to live in God's rest.

$$\frac{1}{\pi} = \frac{2\sqrt{2}}{9801} \sum_{k=0}^{\infty} \frac{(4k)!(1103 + 26390k)}{(k!)^4 396^{4k}}$$

The Infinite Series for Pi

While asleep I had an unusual experience. There was a red screen formed by flowing blood as it were. I was observing it. Suddenly a hand began to write on the screen. I became all attention. That hand wrote a number of results in elliptic integrals. They stuck to my mind. As soon as I woke up, I committed them to writing.
—Srinivasa Ramanujan, mathematician

The dream above is from Srinivasa Ramanujan, the mathematical genius who made brilliant contributions to analytical theory of numbers, elliptical functions, continued fractions, and proved more than 3,000 mathematical theorems in his lifetime. Although Srinivasa did not give credit to God for his dreams, it seems that he was participating with Heaven through the sacrifice (blood) that Jesus made on earth to receive the theorem God was showing him.

Remember: Whether you believe in God or not, He has given you amazing gifts and abilities that He chose to give you and loves it when you benefit from them. *"When God chooses someone and graciously imparts gifts to him, they are never rescinded [taken back or removed]"* (Rom. 11:29).

Learning to Bring Heaven's Creativity to Earth

Thy kingdom come, Thy will be done in earth, as it is in heaven (Matthew 6:10 KJV).

Could it be that God is continually looking for receptive ones to bring what is in Heaven (creativity, art, music, architecture, color, literature, healing, etc.) to earth, using dreams and visions as the method of transfer?

Dreams have been responsible for inventions, solutions to problems, music, stories and concepts for books, movies, and art. Major creative and scientific discoveries have come from dreams. This should cause us to pay close attention to our dreams so God can stir up His gift of creativity in us. The following are examples of dreams from people who may or may not have believed in God but were blessed to receive from His creativity stream.

Science

Dr. James Watson, researcher from Indiana University, dreamed of two intertwined serpents with heads at opposite ends. Some accounts say that he also dreamed of a double-sided staircase. Up until this time (1953) the shape and structure of DNA was not understood, but because of the dreams, Dr. Watson was able to bring this understanding to light.

Albert Einstein, one of the most famous scientists of all time, produced the famous e=mc² theory because of his dreams. The theory asserts that time travel is possible when energy and mass are equivalent and transmutable. In one of his dreams, Einstein was hurtling very fast down a mountainside. As he continued to increase speed he looked up to the sky and saw that the stars began to look differently as he approached the speed of light.

Einstein's theory has triggered countless other theories and plot lines for books and movies because of the ideas and possibilities it opens up for time travel. Einstein learned to take advantage of sleep and napping. He understood that he could solve problems and get ideas when his natural intellect was resting.

Dr. Frederick Banting discovered insulin in his dream and won a Nobel Prize.

One night **Niels Bohr** went to sleep and began dreaming about atoms. He saw the nucleus of the atom, with electrons spinning around it, much as planets spin around their sun. Bohr's dream of atomic structure turned out to be one of the greatest breakthroughs of his day, earning him a Nobel Prize in physics.

Otto Loewi received a Nobel Prize for his contribution to medicine with the discovery that the primary language of nerve cell communication is chemical, not electrical. Here is his dream:

> The night before Easter Sunday of [1920] I awoke, turned on the light and jotted down a few notes on a tiny slip of thin paper. Then I fell asleep again. It occurred to me at 6.00 o'clock in

the morning that during the night I had written down something important, but I was unable to decipher the scrawl. The next night, at 3.00 o'clock, the idea returned.[8]

Music

> God Himself is the creator and music lover, has filled Heaven with it (Job 38:7)! From what we've learned everything in Heaven emanates music in one form or another.
>
> —ANDRAÉ CROUCH

Andraé Crouch was a famous Gospel musician, Grammy winner and songwriter of such classics as "To God be the Glory" and "The Blood Will Never Lose its Power." As a child, Andraé struggled with severe dyslexia and found it difficult to write or read music. He claimed that the gift of music came to him as a fully formed gift when he was 11. He did not have formal music lessons nor did he learn to read music—he simply listened and repeated his creative version of what he heard.

Here is what **Paul McCartney** said about the famous song "Yesterday."

> I woke up with a lovely tune in my head. I thought, That's great, I wonder what that is? ... Because I'd dreamed it I couldn't believe I'd written it. I thought, No, I've never written like this before. But I had the tune, which was the most magic thing.[9]

The song was so complete and real in Paul's dream, he was concerned he was copying someone else work and waited to release the song until he was sure it was unique.

Scientists have found that when a **jazz artist** begins to improvise, the brain behaves similarly when dreaming.

Stravinsky and **Beethoven** heard musical compositions in their dreams. Everything from a fragment of a musical score to an entire canon would appear or be heard in their dreams.

If you've ever woken with a melody or lyrics in your head that you've never heard before, it is possible that you've tapped into Heaven's song, just like Andraé Crouch learned to do even when awake. God is the ultimate creator and may give you a song that touches the world. Write the song out or record it on an audio device.

Literature

Remember, your environment will affect your dreams. The following examples are from writers who have been given amazing stories to tell. Keep in mind that the author has the free will to choose which direction the story will go.

Stuart Little by **E.B. White** was inspired by a dream.

Stephen King, prolific writer and novelist said, "I've always used dreams the way you'd use mirrors to look at something you couldn't see head-on, the way that you use a mirror to look at your hair in the back." He credits his dreams with giving him the concepts for several of his novels and for helping him to solve troublesome story lines.

These popular authors, having received the basic story line from their dreams, have been given amazing gifts—both the talent of writing and the story line. They have also been given free will to choose to bring people life-giving stories or lead them another direction.

There are millions of stories waiting to be written that bring life, joy, and redemption to readers.

Art

Salvador Dalí called many of his works "hand-printed dream photographs."

Movies: There are many movies that have been inspired by dreams, including *Avatar* and *Transformers*, received from dreams in vivid detail by director James Cameron.

Sports: Jack Nicklaus, six-time Masters champion, realized he was gripping his golf club differently in a dream than he did in real life. "I tried it the way I did in the dream and it worked. I feel kind of foolish admitting it, but it really happened in a dream."

Eric Liddell, the great athlete said, "God made me fast, and when I run, I feel His pleasure."

More Inventions

Gary Starkweather, an engineer who invented the laser printer, said: "I believe that to a great extent, the creativity we possess is because the Creator put it there. God put things [in us] as tool developers and creative individuals and I think it has to please Him when He sees us use those faculties to make something completely new."

Mary Hunter, an award-winning inventor and chef, insists all her recipes come from Heaven: "I don't have a cookbook. Prayer is where I get 99 percent of my recipes." She also gives credit to God for her award-winning invention, "Mary's Marinating Stick."

Elias Howe dreamed the solution of how to   improve the sewing machine. Take a look at what you are wearing and you'll realize this invention makes all of our daily lives better.

While in the Presence of Jesus, my friend and author **Anne Elmer** became aware of how we've failed to give God credit for these common household inventions that have

Notes

made our lives so much easier—the doorknob, hairbrush, door hinge, and various garden tools, just to name a few.

When you *give credit and honor to God for a dream*, you participate with bringing Heaven to earth (see Matt. 6:10). You may receive a good earthly reward for your invention, but the best reward will be gained sometime in the future in Heaven and will benefit you for eternity!

38

The King and the Dismembered Hand

38 (30 + 8): **Perfect timing (30); Hebrew for 8: Shah'meyn—eight steps leading to the inner court of the tabernacle, which represents worship—perfect time to worship.**

Daniel and King Belshazzar

God's language tools of interpretation are the same whether you have a dream, a vision, or a supernatural experience. These tools use God's Word as a key to open up understanding as Holy Spirit brings revelation. Here is the biblical story of Daniel, who had the excellent ability to decipher God's thoughts.

King Belshazzar was the leader of Babylon, the most powerful kingdom on earth at the time. To celebrate their victories, the king held a party for over 1,000 people. Food and drink were abundant. At the party, the king demanded *the gold cups and service ware* that had been *stolen from God's temple in Israel* be used to serve food and wine.

During the festivities, Belshazzar began boasting that he was greater than the God of Heaven. He boldly and perversely cursed God and, at the same time, honored his own idols, giving them credit for his success.

Suddenly an unexplainable, supernatural happening took place.

In the middle of the king's arrogant display, a hand (yes, only a hand) began to write on the wall of the room where they were feasting. The hand wrote, "MENE, MENE, TEKEL, UPHARSIN." The words were written in Chaldean, a language understood by the stunned onlookers, but these words made no sense!

The King was terrified! His knees began to shake so hard he could no longer stand. Here is what happened next. The King called his:

- Magicians (use sleight of hand to make impossible things happen, trickery)

- Enchanters (a person who uses spells or magic; a sorcerer or wizard)

- Fortune-tellers (a person who claims to use special powers to tell what will happen to someone in the future)

- Diviners (a person who goes to an evil source to gain information of future events)

Remember: The people in the above list do not go to God for the answers; they tap into the enemy's spirit realm seeking information.

King Belshazzar's mother heard of the panic happening at the party. She came to the king and began to scold him for his absurd and foolish arrogance. Then she said, "There is a man in your kingdom who is full of God's Holy Spirit!

Daniel is well known for his intellectual brilliance and spiritual wisdom. He can be trusted because your father, King Nebuchadnezzar, made him the head of all the magicians, enchanters, fortune-tellers, and diviners. There is no one quite like him. He has a brilliant mind and is incredibly wise. He can do anything—interpret dreams, solve mysteries, explain puzzles. Have Daniel called in. He will tell you what is going on here."

By asking God and listening for His answer, Daniel understood what the words on the wall meant. Daniel had been trained in the Torah (the first five books of the Bible) from a very young age.

Remember: When we read, listen to, and memorize the Word, we will better understand dreams, mysteries and parables as Daniel did.

Here is the interpretation of what the hand wrote on the wall.

- Mene: God has numbered the days of your kingship and brought them to an end.

- Tekel: You and your works have been weighed in the scales and you don't weigh much.

- Peres: Your kingdom has been divided up and handed over to the Medes and Persians.

Daniel's revelation understanding of what God was speaking through the handwriting on the wall was deadly accurate. The entire word came to pass that night. King Belshazzar was murdered and his kingdom was given to the Medes and Persians.[10]

> *Because an extraordinary spirit, knowledge and insight, the ability to interpret*

Notes

dreams, clarify riddles, and solve complex problems were found in this Daniel (Daniel 5:12 AMP).

Famous Dreamers

39 (30 + 9): Perfect + fruitfulness—perfect end.

Famous Biblical Dreamers and Stories about Dreams

Old Testament

Abimelech (Gen. 20:3)

Abraham (Gen. 15:12-13)

Jacob (Gen. 28:10-17; Gen 31:10; Gen. 31:11)

Laban (Gen. 31:24)

Joseph (Gen. 37)

Egyptian butler, baker, and Pharaoh (Gen. 40–41)

The enemy warrior in Gideon's story (Judg. 7)

Saul looked to dreams for answers (1 Sam. 28)

David spoke of dreams in Psalms (Ps. 73:20; 126:1)

Solomon (1 Kings 3:5,15; Eccles. 5:3,7)

Job (Job 7:14; 33:15)

Isaiah speaks of dreams and those who dream (Book of Isaiah)

Jeremiah warns against false dreamers (Jer. 23:28; 29:8)

Daniel (the whole book of Daniel, especially Dan. 5:12)

Nebuchadnezzar (Daniel 2 and 4)

New Testament

Joseph (Matt. 1:20; 2:13; 2:19; 2:22-23)

Wise men (Matt. 2:12)

Pontius Pilate's wife (Matt. 27:19)

Ananias, who baptized Saul/Paul (Acts 9)

Simon Peter and Cornelius (Acts 10 and 11)

Paul (Acts 16:6-10; 18:1-17; 27:22-26)

You! (Joel 2:28; Acts 2:17)

You are never too young or too old to hear from Jesus. You are either *a son* or *a daughter. You* are included in this prophecy that is so important it is repeated in the Old and New Testament.

> *This is what I will do in the last days—I will pour out my Spirit on **everybody** and cause your **sons and daughters to prophesy**, and your **young men will see visions**, and your **old men will experience dreams** from God. The Holy Spirit will come upon **all my servants, men and women alike**, and they will prophesy* (Acts 2:17-18).

Numbers, Names, and Superheroes

40

171717 and My New Address

40: Test, try, and prove.

The number forty is used multiple times in the Bible for time periods—40 days and nights of rain during the flood; Goliath challenged the Hebrew people twice a day for 40 days; forty years represents the time it takes for a new generation to arise.

> In my dream, I **heard** a strong voice and **saw** a hand pointing to the numbers written on what could have been the wall, a page, or in the air. The voice repeated the number **three** times, "17-17-17."
> —STEPH

Details that Jesus emphasizes multiple times or in multiple forms are a strong clue He is working to see that *you do not miss what He has to say*. After this dream, I searched out meaning for the obvious subject, the number 17.

There are multiple ways to consider the interpretation of numbers, as you will see in the chapter on numbers and interpretation. However, none of what I found seemed to satisfy or resolve my curiosity to what Jesus was saying to me.

For days, I would retell the dream to everyone who would listen. One day, when repeating the dream to yet one more friend, I took out a pen and wrote *17 17 17* rather clumsily on a napkin. When I did this, I took a second look at how I had written the numbers. Having studied Hebrew, I was stunned to see—in my own handwriting—the number 17 looked like the Hebrew letter ה, or "hey." Needless to say, this shifted my search to the Hebrew alphabet and the meanings attached to each letter.

Hebrew is an ideogrammatic or "picture" language, along with Chinese, Sumerian, and Egyptian. This means the letters represent or describe a word.

After a brief study of Hebrew letters and the picture they represent, the 17 17 17 dream, or "Hey, Hey, Hey," made more sense to me than anything I had previously considered.

The letter *hey* or ה represents "catching your full attention." When someone says "Hey" to you, especially three times in a row, you purposely focus on what they are trying to say. This applied to current circumstances in my life. I need to pay close attention to not miss this opportunity to participate with His direction and plan.

Jesus was a brilliant storyteller. He teaches everything using literary genius and taps into our own personal characteristics—in this case, my own handwriting helped me hear His thoughts.

One more thought on the Hebrew alphabet:

Psalm 119 is written as an acronym, using a letter of the Hebrew alphabet as the beginning of each section of verses. The Hebrew letters are commonly in our English translations. In researching the above dream, the letter "Hey" refers to the block of verses in Psalm 119:33-40.

If a letter is repeated in your dream, find the equivalent Hebrew letter and correlate it to the verses in Psalm 119 and see if you find additional meaning. The Hebrew letters are commonly available in Psalm 119 in our English Bibles, but just in case, the Bible verses are also included in the dictionary included here.

Get ready—God's way of teaching is not only memorable, it brings lots of joy!

Hebrew Letters and Numbers with Simple Meanings[11]

- **Alef**—1: The head of an ox or bull; strength, leader, or first (Ps. 119:1-8)

- **Bet**—2: A tent or house; family (Ps. 119:9-16)

- **Gimel**—3: Camel or donkey; to lift up, pride, benefit (Ps. 119:17-24)

- **Dalet**—4: Door; pathway, to enter (Ps. 119:25-32)

- **Hey**—5: Behold! to reveal (Ps. 119:33-40)

- **Vav**—6: Nail or peg; to add, to secure (Ps. 119:41-48)

- **Zayin**—7: Weapon; to cut, to cut off (Ps. 119:49-56)

- **Chet**—8: Fence, inner room; private, to separate (Ps. 119:57-64)

- **Tet**—9: Snake; to surround (Ps. 119:65-72)

- **Yood**—10: Closed hand; work, a deed, to make (Ps. 119:73-80)

Notes

- **Kaf**—20: Open hand or palm; to cover, to open, allow (Ps. 119:81-88)

- **Lamed**—30: Cattle goad; control, authority, the tongue (Ps. 119:89-96)

- **Mem**—40: Water; liquid, massive, chaos (Ps. 119:97-104)

- **Noon**—50: Fish darting through the water; activity, life (Ps. 119:105-112)

- **Samech**—60: Prop (such as a walking cane); support, twist slowly, turn (Ps. 119:113-120)

- **Ayin**—70: Eye; to see, know, experience (Ps. 119:121-128)

- **Pey**—80: Mouth; to speak, a word, to open (Ps. 11:129-136)

- **Tsade**—90: Fishhook; catch, desire, need (Ps. 119:137-144)

- **Qoof**—100: Back of the head; behind, the last, the least (Ps. 119:145-152)

- **Reysh**—200: Head of man; a person, the head, the highest (Ps. 119:153-160)

- **Sheen**—300: Teeth; to consume, to destroy (Ps. 119:161-168)

- **Tav**—400: Sign; to seal, to covenant (Ps. 119:169-176)

Names and Specific Details

41: New beginning after a time of trial or testing to find what is true; Strong's Concordance uses the number 41 for Abinadab, or "father of generosity."

Famous actor Matthew McConaughey and his wife, Camila, were choosing names before their first son was born. They considered the name *Matthew Jr.* as a possibility, then learned Levi (or Leviticus) was another name for Matthew in the Bible and carries the same meaning. Matthew McConaughey's favorite verse is Matthew 6:22:

> *The lamp of the body is the eye. If therefore your eye is good [focused correctly on God], your whole body will be full of light* (NKJV).

When the nurse brought the paperwork to fill in the baby's name, the parents realized the time the baby was born was 6:22 P.M., reminding them of Matthew 6:22. This was clear confirmation to Matthew and Camila that the baby's name was Levi!

Your name is important.

God knows your name. Isaiah had an experience with God that gave him understanding of how important you and your name are to God. Even if your

Notes

parents were to forget who you are, God says, *"I'd never forget you—never. Look, I've written your names on the backs of my hands"* (Isa. 49:16 MSG). You are constantly before Jesus's eyes: *"I have called you by your name; you are Mine"* (Isa. 43:1 NKJV).

Names, Dates, Addresses, and Numbers

Just as we don't want to be directed by emotions when interpreting a dream, we want to be careful to not jump to the conclusion that the person in the dream is *literally that person.*

A person who appears in a dream may simply be "playing the part," like an actor, of a *thought or concept* that God is trying to convey to you. For instance, your best friend appears in your dream, but she may be *acting the part* or representing Jesus. Jesus is the best Friend you'll ever have!

When a person appears in your dream, look up their name in a name dictionary. (Check out resources listed in the back of this book.) Step back from what you *think* the dream is about and consider *the name*, separate from what you know about this person. God may surprise you with His thoughts.

A person's name can represent several things:

1. *Character*: their nature or how they are known—happy, sad, grumpy, honest, friendly.

2. *The person's position, role,* or what *they represent to the dreamer*: for instance, a favorite teacher may be in the dream. This teacher may represent *what* they teach—math, science, art—or they could represent Holy Spirit, the

ultimate teacher. A pastor may represent Jesus, the ultimate pastor or shepherd. Remember, people represent a character. They are actors on the stage of our dreams.

3. *The actual meaning* of their names: for instance, *Harley Davidson—Harley* means "favored," *David* means "beloved." The name *Harley Davidson* means "favored and beloved son."

4. Name meanings of *places* such as cities, buildings, parks, and schools may also be significant.

Note: Does your name have a negative meaning attached? Ask God to give you His definition of your name and from this point on use His excellent characterization of who you are.

Intercession Dream

When a dream is about a specific person, it may be Jesus asking you to pray for this person specifically. Do not automatically assume you should tell the person in the dream about the dream, especially if the dream is unsettling.

It is important to learn when to share and when not to. Holy Spirit may share His thoughts so we can agree with Him in prayer for *God's will to be done, on earth as it is in Heaven.* It is an honor to be trusted with God's invitation to pray.

Your first action should be to talk to Jesus about the dream and ask Him for guidance to know what to do. If you are concerned for the person, you may be able to share the dream with a trusted parent, pastor, friend, or leader who

Notes

can agree in prayer with you for God's wisdom and direction. Only share the dream if you know you can safely share (with no hidden agenda) and love is your ultimate goal.

Remember: God always has good things to say. Always look for the good word.

Encourage people, to build them up, and to bring them comfort (1 Corinthians 14:3).

42

Superheroes

42 (40 + 2): Powerful + agreement; (6 x 7 = 42): "His mercy endures forever"—occurs 42 times in Scripture.

> I was in my home surrounded by chaos. Nothing good was happening. I kept trying to do my chores, but as soon as I would get one thing finished, I would turn to find a bigger mess and more chaos. Everything seemed out of control. I looked in the mirror and was shocked to see I had turned into the "Hulk!"
>
> —ETHAN, age 10

Superheroes and Villains

A superhero is one who can manipulate the laws of physics in order to fix an injustice or defeat a villain. Just when the situation seems absolutely impossible, the hero gains or taps into his/her extraordinary strength or power to defeat the villain and stop the havoc he is causing.

Notes

A hero or villain may show up as a metaphor (word picture) in your dream. Jesus is speaking to you in your common language and He is using characters you are familiar with to help you see His thoughts.

Dream Interpretation

In the Hulk story, Bruce Banner is frustrated to the point of intense anger, which makes him morph into a superhuman who has the ability to cause great destruction. At first, Ethan's dream seemed negative.

The key for interpreting this dream was to ask Jesus and seek His heart for Ethan.

After speaking to Ethan about his dream, we learned he had been dealing with anger issues similar to the Hulk. Jesus was helping him see that anger was not the solution but that Jesus wanted to bring peace and self-control (fruit of the Spirit) into his life. Jesus was teaching Ethan—in Ethan's "language."

A "mirror" is a word picture for the Word of God (see 1 Cor. 13:12). When we read or hear the Word, we "see" ourselves better and can correct our actions and ask Jesus for help.

Superheroes have human character traits, both good and bad.

The superheroes we are most familiar with have realized the benefits and drawbacks of their superpowers. If they don't practice their gift, it can be out of control and do great damage.

This is true in real life as well. We have the ability to use the super-gifts and abilities of the Holy Spirit. If the *fruits of the Spirit* (see Gal. 5:22-23; 1 Cor. 13) are not being used in our lives, we can do great damage with *the gifts of the Spirit* (see 1 Cor. 12). There must be balance. Jesus modeled this, and Holy Spirit will help you grow and use these wonderful gifts and tools.

Real people and fictional characters who influence your life are significant.

Jesus is always the best example and ultimate Super-Man. He is able to defeat the enemy and destroy the works of our enemy and worst villain. Jesus rules and reigns with truth, humility, and righteousness. He did *all* He can do to save the world without diminishing our free will.

If you have a superhero dream, remember the *character traits* of the hero and apply them to help understand your dream.

This chapter has dealt with the redemptive or good aspects of familiar superheroes. There are some unrighteous traits that may appear in a dream. Remember, Jesus is using language and characters you are familiar with to convey His message. Jesus is so kind to help us see the problem and help correct our path.

Notes

Jesus has the solution to every super problem. He is the One we are imitating. He is the ultimate superhero!

43

Super Armor

43 (40 + 3): Agreeing with Father, Son, and Holy Spirit and His direction and authority.

The Supernatural Armor we've Been Given is Powerful!

We've been given a "super suit" of armor that God commands us to put on so that *we may stand against every evil* the villain of our soul sends our direction! (See Ephesians 6:10-18.) This super suit is a type of mantle or armor that is better than anything Edna Mode from *The Incredibles* could design.

Here is a list of the pieces of God's armor and the weapons of war that we have been given to use, along with some familiar superheroes who use similar armor and weapons.

Belt of Truth: More effective than Wonder Woman's golden belt or her Lasso of Truth, which expertly extracts information from the enemy.

Our spiritual super-belt brings truth to our thought processes, our attitudes, and our situations and dispels every lie we've believed. One line of truth can set your life on a straight path toward success. God's belt of truth not only speaks truth to you, it helps you declare truth from His Word into every situation. When we know truth, we can boldly proclaim it. Powerful!

Helmet of Salvation: Iron Man, Tony Stark, designed a brilliant interactive helmet and suit. It has an excellent communication piece complete with holograms (pictures/ guidance system).

Holy Spirit gives us supernatural power to see and communicate excellently with God's understanding and ability. The enemy cannot defeat or see inside our God communication (prayer language or praying in the Holy Spirit, Eph. 6:18). God is our ultimate GPS—God Positioning Spirit!

Breastplate of Righteousness: Superman is known as the man of steel and is able to stop any attack with superhuman speed (faster than a speeding bullet) and strength.

Jesus, the ultimate Super-Man, gives us the gift of His righteousness that we wear as strong protection from the fiery darts or "bullets" (words and accusations) from the enemy.

Shield of Faith: Captain America wields his indestructible shield not only as a weapon (offensively) but also as protection (defensively) to stop the enemy's attack.

We are given the shield of faith, which forms a protective barrier around our lives. This protection goes beyond that which we see.

Sword of the Spirit: Although not considered a superhero, the legendary King Arthur was the only one worthy to pull the sword named "Excalibur" from the stone. The character of King Arthur is interesting and he has some attributes that remind us of Jesus, who is the true King of Heaven and Earth. The "stone" can also represent Jesus, who is known as the "rock" in Scripture (see 1 Cor. 10:4). The "sword" (Excalibur) represents the Word, which is embedded in Christ. King Arthur's heart was pure, again representing Jesus.

Wonder Woman also sometimes used a sword, much like the church should be excellent at using God's Word with precision.

Justice League: A community of superheroes is good when the ultimate goal is the same. There is strength in community.

We are a part of the true church; we can learn from and encourage each other. We are running the same race, with similar struggles and pain, and with the ultimate goal of seeing Jesus's Kingdom come and His will be done (see Matt. 6). When we act in love and unity with Jesus and each other, we serve as the true Justice League or the true church.

Don't Stop Here

I hope the list included here has given you a head start into seeing how God loves what we are interested in and He will use our own "language," interests and culture to help us understand His perspective.

Depending on what part of history or literature you are interested in, God will use characters you are familiar with to help you understand His thoughts.

44

3:16 and Your Own Personal Numbers

44: Earth, creation, world—repeated or highlighted; represents division—north, east, south, west; seasons—winter, spring, summer, fall; four gospels.

In huge numbers, the book advertisement on the billboard read "3:16." I sat, waiting at a stoplight, staring at the familiar numbers. I was thinking, "There it is again." Then all of a sudden it hit me! "That is my birthday!" I blurted out loud. March 16 is 3/16. I've been seeing these particular numbers, multiple times almost every day, for years. I had only recently begun to take notice of repeating numbers or symbols. For as long as I can remember, I would wake in the night, look to see the time, and there it would be again—3:16. I would pray, knowing Jesus wanted to speak to me, but I had not associated it closely with my life other than the Bible verse John 3:16. I now realize the connection these numbers have to my birth, amplifying how much Jesus loves and cares about every detail about my life.

Hidden Treasure: Your Own Personal Numbers

The number 316, which happens to be my birthday (March 16) is the most commonly seen number in my life. This number is prominent daily—so much so, I finally asked Jesus why. He simply said, "Stephanie, you need to know how much I love you." This is true for all of us.

As you practice interpreting your dreams, you will develop your own unique "language" with God. As you connect with various numbers, words, repeating symbols, and pictures, your vocabulary grows and how Jesus is speaking uniquely to you becomes clearer. It is like having a secret code with God.

> *For this is how much God loved the world—*
> *he gave his one and only, unique Son as a gift.*
> *So now everyone who believes in him will*
> *never perish but experience everlasting life*
> (John 3:16).

3:16[12]

When I see these particular numbers, I know Jesus is reminding me of His love. Other times these same numbers have encouraged me to keep going no matter what the circumstances are and to keep loving others even when they do not return that love. The more I see these numbers, the more I love how He speaks to me.

On a recent missions trip to Nepal, the numbers 11:11 and 1:11 and 11 began reoccurring daily. The repeating number *one* was an easy trigger, so we searched the Scriptures, easily finding what we were to declare over our time and ministry in the country. During the entire trip we found confidence each time the numbers reappeared, knowing God was directing us and was working alongside us to accomplish everything we were in the country to establish.

By communicating in this way, God is strengthening His relationship with us. He wants us to hear His gentle voice in a number as much as He wants us to see a very obvious, brilliant double rainbow splashed across the sky or hear His exclamation of strength in the crash of thunder.

Tool: Use a website such as BibleGateway.com to search the Scriptures for the numbers of your birthday or other numbers you see repeatedly in your life.

When you see a word, symbol, or number, especially one that is repeated in your life:

- **Ask Holy Spirit** what this means for you and welcome His help in learning the significance.

- **Do some research** by using your Bible, a dictionary, thesaurus, or computer search to find out the number or symbol's significance.

- **Use a trusted dream dictionary** as recommended in the bibliography at the end of this book.

- **Do a word study** of the original Hebrew meaning.

- **Check Strong's Concordance:** This is a good tool to look up numbers that associate with Hebrew words and their meanings.

- **Do historical research.** It is possible that the day you have a dream has significance. Research what has happened on this day,

Notes

Notes

not only historically but see if there is a connection to your personal life history.

God is creative beyond our imagination, so it is best to not become set on just one meaning. Jesus loves it when we keep pursuing Him to find new understanding. Your individuality, personality, and culture all will add meaning to your understanding of numbers. Just as there are deeper meanings in God's Word when we search out the Scriptures, you'll learn to find deeper meaning in what He is speaking to you.

You may find it becomes a bunch of fun to see what numbers show up in your life. The digital clock numbers seen repeatedly, a test score, the mileage odometer in your vehicle, a store receipt total, a dream where someone hands you a check with numbers on it. Numbers typically show up without expectation on our part, so when they repeat or show a pattern it is a fun way of developing conversation, language, and relationship just between you and Jesus.

45

More on Numbers

45 (40 + 5): Undergoing testing and trials with the grace of God followed by reawakening.

Edwin Moses, an Olympic hurdler from the US, was in Koblenz, West Germany in August of 1983. He was so relaxed before the event he forgot to take off his wristwatch. Moses ran the 400-meter hurdle race like a well-oiled machine and broke the world record by .11 of a second. Afterward, Moses said that before the race he had recurring dreams involving sets of numbers. The numbers he had dreamed were "8-31-83," Moses's birthday (8/31 or August 31) *and* the date of this famous race in Germany. He also saw the numbers "4703," which Moses actually surpassed, winning the race with a time of 47.02.

Numbers in a Dream

- A number may simply refer to the literal number.

- Numbers can be a divider or multiplier. Example: 120 may be the combined meanings of 10 and 12 because ten multiplied by twelve is 120.

- Addition or subtraction: 120 may be 100 + 20 or even adding the digits 1 + 2 = 3.

- Numbers can be put together multiple ways. You can look up one number, grasp its meaning, then know that the multiplier magnifies the thought.

Any number can be God's *specific love language* to you. Numbers show up in multiple ways and can become a type of treasure hunt.

- Your birthday, birth year, adoption day, or any other important date in your life.

- The numbers in a person's address can be used as a way to pray for or bless that home. For instance, a neighbor's house number may be 555, so speaking, "grace, grace, grace," one of the meanings of the number 5, would be in agreement with the number established over their home.

- License plate numbers to know how to pray for the person in that car on the highway.

- Numbers on the clock.

- Pay attention to any number that shows up multiple times in your life and use a good definition of that number to remind yourself how much Jesus loves you.

- A goal number, like Edwin Moses's dream above, may be seen in multiple ways so that you can be reminded to focus and encouraged to future success.

The chapters in this book begin with the number and its definition. Use *The Divinity Code To Understanding Your Dreams and Visions* for fuller understanding on numbers.

Larger Numbers Defined

- 0: May represent God.

- 50: Jubilee; liberty, freedom.

- 100: Complete completeness, 10 x 10; maximum blessing.

- **1,000:** Ever increasing, or more. If the number is greater, consider the number meaning on its own with the understanding it is increasing or being multiplied or magnified. For instance, 8,888 = abundant new beginning, multiplied and repeated!

- 5,000: Ever increasing grace.

- 10,000: The maximum possible in earthy terms; extreme.

If you see a number repeating regularly, ask Jesus what He is saying. His answer will be the surest answer to your situation. God's reasoning for the number will fit perfectly into your life calling, your personality, your culture, and your understanding.

Notes

Final Notes

46

Who Is Jesus?

Knowing God and His Love for You

- God created you (Gen. 1:1-27).

- He knew you before you were conceived and planned the time you would be born and the number of days you would live on earth (Ps. 139:13-14).

- God called you by name (Isa. 43:1; 49:16).

- God wrote your name on His hand because He wants to see your name always (Isa. 49:16).

- God considers you lovely and handsome. He loves how He made you, every detail (Song of Songs).

- You are His expression, His explanation of what love is on the earth (Ps. 139).

- God knows and loves your personality. He knows your thoughts before you think them and He loves watching you speak, sing, laugh, play, learn, and sleep.

- He never tires of being with you and keeps speaking to you even when you sleep (Job 33:13-14).

Notes

- He is always thinking good thoughts about you and saying good things about you.

- He is closer to you than your own breath (Phil. 4:5).

- He knows what words you'll say before you say them (Ps. 139:1-4).

- God has a brilliant plan for you (Jer. 29:11).

- God is always for you and for your success (Jer. 29:11).

- He wants you to have the best life possible (John 10:10).

- When you do wrong things or hurt someone, He provided for freedom from guilt and wants you to run to Him for everything you need. Never run from Him; He always wants to see you and talk to you (Rom. 3:22; Isa. 1:18).

- God cannot even think of rejecting you (Ps. 27:10).

- He loved you so much, He left Heaven so that He could make it possible for you to be with Him forever (Rom. 5:8).

- He wanted to know what it is like to be on the earth and live like you do.

- He wanted to experience everything that you may see, or do, or have to endure (John 3:16).

- God knows and cares for the tiniest bird. He will always supply your needs (Matt. 6:26).

- His love for you reaches the distance from here to Heaven, immeasurable in our understanding (Ps. 103:11-12).

- When you ask His forgiveness, He sends your wrongdoing as far as the east is from the west. So far away, even He forgets where it is (Ps. 103:11-12).

- You are His prized possession, His ultimate treasure. He asked God the Father for you for His inheritance.

- He desires your friendship more than His own life.

Notes

The most wonderful words you can say to Him are, "I choose You, Jesus."

47

What Is Prayer?

Here is my favorite way to pray:

"Here I am Jesus—the one You love."

When you listen, Jesus says in return, "Here I Am, the One *you* love."

Prayer is simply talking to Jesus. He is always listening and will speak to you as you listen.

When you feel no love or acceptance from anyone else, you can confidently know you are deeply loved and accepted by Jesus.

Do you know there are many people praying for you?

I am one of them. Many times, Jesus wakes me (and countless other people) in the night or reminds us during the day. Jesus lets us know that He simply needs our agreement with Him for what you and others all over the world are enduring. Be confident—you are in someone's prayer.

You are never alone.

Most importantly, Jesus Himself is praying for you!

He is always talking to the Father saying, "I see what (put your name here) is doing; I see how she/he is struggling, how much she/he loves me. I see the difficulty. I see the good and know the potential and abilities he/she carries. Here is what he/she needs, Father…."

Jesus is the *great* Mediator, standing *with* you and fighting for you and has the very best plan for your life.

Always *Remember*:

- God holds the universe.

- He holds your heart.

- He holds your hand.

- He knows and loves every single detail about you.

- He loves you every single second of every single day.

- There is nothing you can do to make Him love you more—or less. You truly are His favorite one.

Notes

48

Why Should I Read the Bible?

The Ancient Books of Wisdom and Dreams

The most important collection of books you will ever read is the Word of God, the Bible.

This book carries profound truth, where one sentence can change your life forever. No other book in the history of earth has been so life-changing and continually relevant. If you pick up your Bible today, you'll find it has more solid truth and good information than any newspaper available, and where a newspaper is outdated before the day is over, God's Word has stood the test of time and will continue to throughout eternity.

The late John Paul Jackson taught that one-third of Scripture records actual dreams or the story of the dreams coming to pass. If God used this much available space in the Word to record dreams, should we not much more carefully consider how He speaks to us in dreams?

Dream interpretation becomes easier as you read your Bible. The keys to understanding are right in the Word.

The more I read God's Word, the more I learn and the more I realize how much I do not know. Beloved Pastor Boulware used to say, "The Word of God is so vast it is like trying to empty the ocean with a teaspoon."

This same pastor taught us to read our Bible through, cover to cover, every year. He would read completely through his Bible every quarter (three months) and had read through over 100 times. I began this habit in my early 20s and continued through life. It has been the one continuous stabilizing factor in my life for decades. Even when I could not dream of making it through in a year because of life circumstances, somehow I always did.

Enjoyable Bible Reading

I learned to make reading the Word fun, and I would challenge myself to make it to certain goals daily, monthly, or yearly.

Here are some tips for yearly reading:

- Divide the total number of pages in your Bible by the number of days in a year, which typically comes to about five pages. With this in mind, the goal may be to read at least five pages a day.

- For the very difficult and not so interesting parts, speed-read through to not get discouraged or sidetracked.

- Audio Bibles are wonderful! Hearing the Word is powerful.

- Chose whatever translation you are happy with. It is fun to change versions each year.

- No matter what your age, I recommend a large-print Bible. Large print makes

Notes

Notes

reading faster and easier and puts less strain on your eyes.

- When possible, binge read. Set a goal of reading an entire book in one sitting. This is easy in the New Testament but a challenge in the Old Testament. This goal will help you get ahead in your goal for reading and will also give you a new perspective of the book you are reading beginning to end.

- The books that seem too boring or slow can be quickly read in one sitting, so as not to get stuck.

- Habits take about 40 days to form.

- At first it may be "crunchy" and slow; however, you'll soon learn how important it really is and reading and hearing the Word becomes sweeter as the years pass.

- The Word renews your mind—like a bath for your thoughts.

*Every Scripture has been written by the Holy Spirit, the breath of God. It will empower you by its **instruction** and **correction**, **giving you the strength** to take the **right direction** and lead you deeper into the path of godliness. Then you will be God's servant, fully **mature** and **perfectly prepared** to fulfill any assignment God gives you* (2 Timothy 3:16-17).

Reading versus Study

Note: the goal here is to encourage Bible *reading*; Bible *study* is different but also important. Bible study adds context and depth to your reading. Study will improve your understanding of topics and will make your Bible reading more enjoyable; however, while you are reading don't get sidetracked on study (unless you have the time) as it may stop your progress.

The wonderful benefit of reading through your entire Bible is that you'll get a brilliant overview perspective of the entire Word of God.

This is important because many times we hear small parts of Scripture and not the full story behind it. Trivia games that use Scripture for questions are more interesting and easier when you understand the whole Bible instead of just snippets of Scripture.

When people ask me questions or need counsel, many times I'll get a much-needed wise answer that I know did not come from me but was available because I've read my Bible so many times. The principleof biblical knowledge, the historical timeline, along with precious wisdom become available when we invest our time in God's Word.

> *A joyous blessing rests upon the one **who reads** this message and upon those **who hear** and embrace the words of this prophecy* (Revelation 1:3).

Reward Yourself for Completion

Keep track of how many times you read. Use hash marks to keep a tally or simply list the year finished. This helps with goal setting. I'm almost to 40 times and looking forward

Notes

to 100 times completely through the Bible. At first it was difficult to make it through one time a year; now I can accomplish two or three times a year.

When finished, **reward** yourself for an amazing accomplishment. If you are young, ask your parent or pastor if there might be a reward to help you complete this goal—a new set of colored pencils or highlighters for the next reading or a new Bible for a fresh start.

Journaling: Writing out an entire book of the Bible can be very enjoyable. The more we participate with the Word by reading, writing, hearing, and doing, the more the Word becomes personal, real, and usable.

A final Note: *No* legalism. Do not allow yourself to become a slave to reading or listening; instead, become a friend of the Word. Jesus will help—just ask.

> *Your extravagant kindness to me makes me want to follow your words even more!* (Psalm 119:65)

49

What Is Fire Camp?

We believe it is important to have opportunities to encounter the love of Jesus as a child. This will set children on a path of lifelong pursuit after the One we love.

Fire Camp began as such an opportunity. During the camp, our goal is to learn and safely practice the supernatural tools of the Holy Spirit (prophecy, dreams, healing, and creativity), endeavoring to build up and strengthen each other (the church) by tapping into Heaven's resources for healing, encouragement, and creativity.

Fire Camp has grown to include people of all ages, giving a safe place to use and practice the gifts of the Spirit as we prepare for the great harvest to come. Regardless of age, we have the opportunity to participate with Heaven:

> *My speech and my preaching were not with persuasive words of*
> *human wisdom, but in demonstration of the Spirit and of power*
> (1 Corinthians 2:4 NKJV).

Fire Camp is an opportunity to encounter Jesus and learn and safely practice using the supernatural tools of the Holy Spirit. It is the normal believer's life to work with Jesus to make it possible for His Kingdom to come and His will to be done on earth as it is in Heaven (see Matt. 6:9-13).

Fire Camp Focuses on Five Topics

1. **How to hear Jesus's voice**: The prophetic is an invitation to listen and participate with Heaven.

2. **Healing**: Pain and sickness is an invitation for the miracle healing power of Jesus.

3. **Art and creativity**: Working with Heaven's creative resources to bring prophetic pictures, healing, and comfort in visual form.

4. **Dreams and dream interpretation**: A dream is an opportunity to gain wisdom from God's perspective in a dream parable.

5. **Angels** accompany us in our everyday lives and to do the work of the Kingdom. We receive help and encouragement transported by the angelic from Heaven.

Every camp is different and it is the goal of our team to be as flexible as possible with particular leadership desires.

Option: The key to lasting revival among our young people is setting them on a foundation of God's Word that *does not deny them access to or ignore* the true biblical supernatural.

If we neglect to train our young people in the supernatural, the dark side will, twisting their gifts and robbing them of His pleasures here and an eternity separated from His goodness.

Please contact Stephanie with questions or for an invitation:

Email: Stephanie@woodsource.com

Website: www.dwellingplace-events.com

Recommended Reading

Here I Am, the One You Love, takes you gently through a supernatural day in the life of a child living the normal Christian life. The author leads the reader with scriptural principles that are mature but easily grasped by children. The prophetic illustrations draw you into the Presence of Jesus as you soak in His love.

Topics: God's love for you, forgiveness, repeating God's Word until it becomes a part of you, agreeing with God and His Word, dreams, visions, sensing God's Presence, and hearing God's heart for yourself.

The prevailing theme of *Here I Am, the One You Love* is to remind you of how deeply you are loved by God and that you are never too old to be His child.

Beautifully illustrated hardcover edition available at Amazon.

Here I Am, the One You Love, written by Stephanie Schureman, illustrated by Lori Vafiades, 2011, Dwelling Place Press, Golden, Co. www .dwellingplacepress.com.

Resources

There are many excellent resources on dreams from trusted ministries included here. The books I most highly recommend are *The Divinity Code to Understanding Your Dreams and Visions* and *God's Prophetic Symbolism in Everyday Life*, both by Adam Thompson and Adrian Beale, published by Destiny Image Publishing, www.thedivinitycode.org.

Dreams are a gift. The ability to interpret dreams is our inheritance, part of the normal Christian life.

These books have thorough metaphor dictionaries that tie word pictures to Scripture and further explain dreams from a Spirit-led, biblical basis. The examples and teaching Adrian and Adam give are life giving and build solid footing so that you can confidently interpret dreams with the Word's guidance, following the direction of the Holy Spirit.

The Divinity Code to Understanding your Dreams and Visions contains:

- Excellent teaching on dreams, visions, and supernatural experiences.
- The most extensive Christian dream metaphor dictionary on the market.
- Over 3,000 metaphors, each meticulously tied to Scripture.
- An additional dictionary of names and places.
- 101 interpreted dreams providing credible evidence.

One of the best books available on dreams and dream interpretation.

The Divinity Code to Understanding Your Dreams and Visions by Adrian Beale and Adam F. Thompson, Destiny Image Publishers, Shippensburg, PA. Highly recommended.

Online, www.BehindtheName.com is a wonderful resource for searching out first and last names, as well as place names.

The Name Book: Over 10,000 Names, Their Meanings, Origins, and Spiritual Significance by Dorothy Astoria, Bethany House publishers, 2008.

Hearing God:. for Intimacy, Healing, Creativity, Meditation and Dream Interpretation" by Mark and Patti Virkler, 2014; published by Destiny Image, Shippensburg, PA, 2014.

Understanding Dreams and Visions by John Paul Jackson, Flower Mound, TX, Streams Ministries International, 2014. Http://www.streamsministries.com has a huge number of quality resources for understanding dreams. Highly recommended.

Hebrew Word Pictures: How does the Hebrew Alphabet Reveal Prophetic Truths? by Dr. Frank T. Seekins, published by Hebrew World. This and many other excellent Hebrew learning tools are available at http://www.hebrew1.com. Highly recommended.

Do Our Pets Go to Heaven? by Terry James and other contributors, published by Defender, Crane, MO, 2013.

For difficult issues, the series of books titled, "Starved," "Cut, " "Violated," or "Trapped," by Nancy Alcorn of Mercy Ministries are helpful. Order at www.mercyministries.com.

Powerful book for families to read:

Visions Beyond the Veil by H.A Baker, published by Whitaker House, 2006.

The Prophetic Voice of God: Learning to Recognize the Language of the Holy Spirit by Lana Vawser, Destiny Image Publishers

Notes

Notes

1. James W. Goll, Lou Engle, *The Call of the Elijah Revolution*, (Shippensburg, PA: Destiny Image Publishers, 2011), 101.

2. For a more extensive study of numbers, the author recommends *The Divinity Code to Understanding Your Dreams and Visions*, and *God's Prophetic Symbolism in Everyday Life* by Adrian Beale and Adam F. Thompson.

3. Cory Asbury, "Reckless Love," from *Reckless Love*, Bethel Music 2018.

4. Albert Hammond and Carole Bayer Sager, "When I Need You," sung by Leo Sayer, Sony/ATV Music Publishing LLC, Warner/Chappell Music, Inc., Carlin America Inc., 1977.

5. Jennifer LeClaire, "A Warning to Preachers Engaging in Ministry Espionage," Jennifer LeClaire Ministries, March 21, 2018, https://jenniferleclaire.org/articles/warning-preachers-engaging-ministry-espionage/.

6. Patricia King, *Developing Your Five Spiritual Senses* (XP Publishing, 2014).

7. Aristotle, *The History of Animals*, The Internet Classics Archive, Book IV, part 10, accessed June 26, 2018, http://classics.mit.edu/Aristotle/history_anim.html.

8. Alli N. McCoy and Siang Yong Tan, "Otto Loewi (1873–1961): Dreamer and Nobel Laureate," *Singapore Medical Journal* 55, no. 01 (January 2014), doi:10.11622/smedj.2014002.

9. Barry Miles, *Paul McCartney: Many Years from Now* (New York: H. Holt, 1998), 201-202.

10. This chapter modified from Daniel 5 in *The Message Bible*.

11. For a more complete study, see Dr. Frank T. Seekins, *Hebrew Word Pictures: How Does the Hebrew Alphabet Reveal Prophetic Truths?* available at http://www.hebrew1.com.

12. Max Lucado, *3:16, The Numbers of Hope* (Nashville, TN: Thomas Nelson Publishing, 2009).

About Stephanie Schureman

Stephanie Schureman, author, speaker, and founder of Dwelling Place Ministries is an ordained minister and teacher at two local Bible schools. Stephanie leads conferences and prophetic/revival equipping *Fire Camp* for children, youth, and adults and has authored *Here I Am, the One You Love*. Stephanie is a homeschooling mother of six children, blessed with five grandchildren, and the wife of husband Cris for over thirty-five years, residing in Golden, Colorado.

OTHER BOOKS BY STEPHANIE SCHUREMAN

Here I Am, the One You Love